Nelson Thornes Shakespeare

The Tempest

Volume editor: **David Stone**

Series editors: **Duncan Beal and Dinah Jurksaitis**

Series consultant: **Peter Thomas**

Published in 2003 by:
Nelson Thornes Ltd
Delta Place
27 Bath Road
CHELTENHAM
GL53 7TH
United Kingdom

03 04 05 06 07 / 10 9 8 7 6 5 4 3 2 1

A catalogue record for this book is available from the British Library

ISBN 0 7487 6957 7

Page make-up by Tech-Set

Printed and bound in Spain by Graphycems

Acknowledgements

Mary Evans Picture Library: p4, p14; Shakespeare Birthplace Trust: p10, p11, p60, p78, p96, p116

Contents

Preface

The very name *Shakespeare* can overwhelm: so many associations with culture and history. We hope you will approach the plays with curiosity and a willingness to embrace the strangeness of Shakespeare's world: those quaint ways, weapons and words!

Our aim in the **Nelson Thornes Shakespeare** series is to provide a bridge between Shakespeare's world, and our own. For all the differences between the two worlds it is intriguing to find so many similarities: parents and children; power games; loyalty and treachery; prejudice; love and hate; fantasy and reality; comedy and horror; the extremes of human behaviour. It is oddly moving to find that the concerns of the human race have not changed so much over the centuries, and that Shakespeare's themes are modern and recognisable.

The unfamiliarity of the language is best regarded not as a barrier, but as a source of interest. On the left-hand pages we have not only explained unfamiliar words, but have also drawn attention to aspects of wordplay, imagery and verse. The left-hand pages also have reminders that this is a piece of theatre, written to be performed and experienced visually. The **performance features** boxes invite you to consider such questions as: *How might this character react? What actions might be appropriate here? Try reading/acting this section in this way...* You are not fed one interpretation; you make the decisions.

To help you place individual scenes in the context of the whole play there is a **comparison feature** at the end of each scene: *Where else have we seen characters behaving like this? How do events in this scene parallel events two scenes back?* A brief **scene summary** brings together the main developments within that scene.

At the beginning of the play there are some **introductory essays** on background topics. They highlight aspects of Shakespeare's world which show a different outlook to our own: *How did they conduct courtship in his day? How has the status of the monarchy changed? What about their view of magic and the supernatural?*

A separate **Teacher Resource Book** contains material which will help deepen your understanding of the play. There are **worksheets** on individual scenes – valuable if you have missed any of the class study. They will also provide a good background which will help you demonstrate your knowledge in coursework essays. To this end, the book also contains some **Coursework Assignment essay titles** and hints on how to tackle them. The play and resource book together provide enough support to allow you to study independently, and to select the assignment you want to do, rather than all working together as a class.

Our aim is that you finish the play enthused and intrigued, and eager to explore more of Shakespeare's works. We hope you will begin to see that although ideally the plays are experienced in performance, there is also a place for reading together and discussing as a class, or for simply reading them privately to yourself.

Foreword

Who bothers to read introductions, especially introductions to plays by Shakespeare?

Well, you do, obviously, and that's a good start if you want to get more from your literature study. Reading this Foreword will help you to get more from Shakespeare's writing and from the accompanying material provided with the play.

Shakespeare – the great adapter

Shakespeare is regarded as a great writer but not because he was an original inventor of stories. His plays are nearly all adaptations of stories he found in books, or in history – or in somebody else's play. His originality came from the way he used this material. He changed his sources to suit himself and his audiences and was never afraid to change the facts if they didn't suit him.

The best way of understanding what Shakespeare thought valuable in a story is to look at the way he altered what he found.

The **Introductory essays** show how he changed characters or time-scales to enhance the dramatic effect or to suit a small cast of actors.

Shakespeare – the great realist

What Shakespeare added to his source material was his insight into people and society. He understood what makes people tick and what makes society hold together or fall apart. He showed how people behave – and why – by showing their motives and their reactions to experiences such as love, loss, dreams, fears, threats and doubts. These have not changed, even if we think science and technology make us different from people in Shakespeare's day. He was also realistic. He avoided stereotypes, preferring to show people as a complex mixture of changing emotions.

When you use the character sheets provided by your teacher, you will see this realism in action. His characters behave differently in different circumstances, and they change over time – just as we do in real life.

Shakespeare – the language magician

Shakespeare's cleverness with language is not just his ability to write beautiful poetry. He also wrote amusing dialogue, common slang, rude insults and the thoughts of people under pressure. He wrote script that uses the sounds of words to convey emotion, and the associations of words to create vivid images in our heads.

When you use the glossary notes you will see how his language expresses ugliness, hatred, suspicion, doubt and fear as well as happiness, beauty and joy.

Shakespeare – the theatrical innovator

Theatre before Shakespeare was different from today. Ordinary people enjoyed songs and simple shows, and educated people – the minority – enjoyed stories from Latin and Greek. Moral and religious drama taught right and wrong and there were spectacular masques full of music and dance for the audience to join in. Shakespeare put many of these elements together, so most people could expect something to appeal to them. He was a comprehensive writer for a comprehensive audience, writing to please the educated and the uneducated. He was the first to put realistic people from every walk of life on stage – not just kings and generals, but characters who talked and behaved like the ordinary folk in the audience. He was less interested in right and wrong than in the comedy or tragedy of what people actually do. *Only Fools and Horses*, and *Eastenders*, are dramas which follow a trend started by Shakespeare over four hundred years ago. He managed this in theatres which lacked lighting, sound amplification, scene changes, curtains or a large cast of actors.

The performance features accompanying the play text will help to show you how Shakespeare's stagecraft is used to best dramatic effect.

Whether you are studying for GCSE or AS, the examination is designed to test your ability to respond to the following:

1 Shakespeare's ideas and themes
2 Shakespeare's use of language
3 Shakespeare's skill in writing for stage performance
4 The social, cultural and historical aspects of his plays
5 Different interpretations of the plays.

1a. Showing personalities (ideas and themes)

Shakespeare thought drama should do more than preach simple moral lessons. He thought it should show life as it was, daft and serious, joyful and painful. He didn't believe in simple versions of good and evil, heroes and villains. He thought most heroes had unpleasant parts to their nature, just as most villains had good parts. This is why he showed people as a mixture. In *Hamlet*, he wrote that the dramatist should **hold a mirror up to nature**, so that all of us can see ourselves reflected. As he picks on the parts of human behaviour that don't change (fear, jealousy, doubt, self-pity), his characters remind us of people we know today – and of ourselves – not just people who lived a long time ago. This is because Shakespeare shows us more than his characters' status in life. He knew that beneath the robes or the crown there is a heart the same as any tradesman's or poor person's. He knew that nobody in real life is perfect – so he didn't put perfect characters on his stage.

As a hero, Prospero has magic powers and wants revenge for the injustice done to him, but shows mercy when his enemies are in his power. He is not completely virtuous however – he can be bad tempered and cruel at times, quite willing to treat Caliban like a slave.

1b. Showing what society was/is like (ideas and themes)

In *Hamlet*, Shakespeare declared that drama should show the **form and pressure of the age**, meaning the structure of the times we live in and the pressures and influences it creates.

Elizabethan England had known great conflict and turmoil through civil unrest and was also always under threat from other countries (Shakespeare was 20 at the time of the Spanish Armada). It was also a nation changing from the old ways of country living. London and other cities were growing, and voyagers were exploring other lands. New trades were developing, and plague and disease spread quickly in crowded parts of the cities. Most people were superstitious, but science was beginning to make its mark. People still generally believed in the Divine Right of Kings, but they were beginning to think that bad kings may be removed for the country's good. One such example was Charles I who was executed only 33 years after Shakespeare's death.

In *The Tempest* there are new ideas about kingship and the causes of rebellion, ideas about the New World and whether civilisation is a result of nature or nurture.

2. Shakespeare's use of the English language (sound and image)

Shakespeare wrote the speech of uneducated servants and traders but he could also write great speeches using rhetoric. Whether it is a dim-witted inn-servant called Francis in *Henry IV Part One*, or a subtle political operator like Mark Antony in *Julius Caesar*, Shakespeare finds words to make them sound and seem convincing.

To show Prospero moved into fury by the behaviour of Caliban, Shakespeare fills his speech full with harsh consonants, rough 'r' sounds and 'h' sounds (aspirates) to help the actor: **Hag-seed – hence! … Shrugst thou? … I'll rack thee with old cramps … make thee roar**.

3a. Writing for a mixed audience (writing for stage performance)

As a popular dramatist who made his money by appealing to the widest range of people, Shakespeare knew that some of his audience would be literate, and some not. So he made sure that there was something for everybody – something clever and something vulgar, something comic and something tragic.

In *The Tempest* there is morality, philosophy and farce (drunkenness, and shenanigans under the gabardine) as well as spectacle – music, dance and the masque.

3b. Shakespeare's craft (writing for stage performance)

Shakespeare worked with very basic stage technology but, as a former actor, he knew how to give his actors the guidance they needed. His scripts use embedded prompts, either to actors, or to the audience, so that he did not have to write stage directions for his actors. If an actor says, **Put your cap to its proper purpose**, it is a cue to another actor to be using his hat for fancy gestures, rather than wearing it on his head. If an actor comes on stage and says, **So this is the forest of Arden** we know where the scene is set, without expensive props and scenery.

In *The Tempest*, there are storm effects, partly because when he wrote it he had moved to the indoor Blackfriars theatre, which had lighting and more sound effects machinery than he was used to.

4. Social, cultural and historical aspects

There are two ways of approaching this. One way is to look at what the plays reveal for us about life in Shakespeare's time – and how it is different from today. The other is to look at what the plays reveal for us about life in Shakespeare's time – and how it is the same today.

If you learn from *The Tempest* that people who wrap themselves up in study tend to be taken advantage of by others who don't act fairly, you can ask if this may be true today.

5. Alternative interpretations

You can look at Shakespeare's play in its own time and in ours and sometimes see differences, and sometimes see similarities. Your literature study expects you to understand how Shakespeare can be interpreted by different people in different eras and in different places. It's important to have your own view of how the plays should be performed.

The notes and commentary throughout this edition will help you to form your own interpretation, and to understand how others might interpret differently. Look especially at references to how different stage and film productions have taken different approaches to the script that Shakespeare wrote.

Enjoy Shakespeare's play! It's your play, too!

Peter Thomas

Introductory essays

Shakespeare's sources

There is no single source for *The Tempest*. Shakespeare did not adapt or draw upon one particular story or historical event as he did for some of his other plays. Instead, he found inspiration from a number of places. The most important of these were the following: a letter written in 1610 by William Strachey, which described the shipwreck of the *Sea Venture*; an essay written by Michel Eyquem de Montaigne entitled *Of the Caniballes* (see page 7); Virgil's *Aeneid* and Ovid's *Metamorphoses*. It is also likely that Shakespeare knew 'Mirror of Knighthood', a Spanish romance translated between 1580 and 1586 which contains some elements of plot and setting similar to those found in *The Tempest*.

A real tempest and shipwreck: William Strachey's A True Reportory

On 2 June 1609, a fleet of nine ships, with 600 people on board, set out from England bound for the new English colony in Virginia. The *Sea Venture* carried the newly appointed governor of the colony, Sir Thomas Gates, and Sir George Somers, Admiral of the Virginia Company. On 25 July, with 'the cloudes gathering thick upon us, and the windes singing, and whistling most unusually', a storm battered the ships for several days. After the storm eased, four of the ships re-formed and sailed on to Virginia to be joined, eventually, by three more. The *Sea Venture* did not arrive and was presumed to be lost. In fact the ship had run aground, after receiving 'a mighty leake', on the 'dangerous and dreaded llands of the Bermuda'. The reputation of this place as 'given over to Devils and wicked Spirits' was contrary to what the colonists found, and they lived there for some nine months while building another ship under Somers's direction. On 10 May 1610, they proceeded to their destination, reaching Jamestown, Virginia, two weeks later.

The report of the loss of the *Sea Venture* and of Sir Thomas Gates had caused a sensation in England and the news of their survival caused another. Several accounts of the story were published in late 1610: the first of these was *A Discovery of the Bermudas* by Sylvester Jourdain; another was *A True Declaration of the Estate of the Colonie in Virginia*, published on behalf of the Virginia Company; and the most important was William Strachey's *A True Reportory of the Wrake, and Redemption of Sir Thomas Gates* which, though not published until 1625, is dated 15 July 1610. Strachey's account, in the form of a letter, was addressed to an unidentified lady.

Shakespeare would certainly have had easy access to the published accounts of the adventure, which appeared in 1610, a year before the first performance of *The Tempest*. He also had numerous connections with William Strachey through mutual friends who were involved with the Virginia Company, and to Strachey himself, who was interested in the London theatre.

There are many cross-references between Strachey's account and the text. Here are just a few examples from a number of points in the play.

- Strachey writes that the storm is 'roaring' and 'beat all light from heaven; which like an hell of darkness turned black upon us … The sea swelled above the clouds which gave battel unto heaven'.

  Miranda says to Prospero:

  > **'… you have**
  > **Put the wild waters in this roar …**
  > **The sky it seems would pour down stinking pitch**
  > **But that the sea, mounting to the welkin's cheek,**
  > **Dashes the fire out.'** *(Act 1 Scene 2, lines 1–5)*

- Strachey says that, 'Our clamours drouned in the windes, and the windes in thunder. Prayers … drowned in the outcries of the officers'.

  The Boatswain says,

  > **'A plague upon this howling. They are louder than the**
  > **weather, or our / office.'** *(Act 1 Scene 1, lines 30–1)*

- Strachey relates how the sailors 'threw over-boord much luggage … and staved many a butt of Beers … wine and vinegar'.

  Stephano boasts that he

  > **'escaped upon a butt of sack, which the / sailors heaved**
  > **o'erboard'** *(Act 2 Scene 2, lines 97–8)*.

- When describing the island, Strachey tells of 'high sweet-smelling woods' but also writes of 'Fennes, Marishes, Ditches, muddy pools'.

  In the play, Adrian remarks that **'The air breathes upon us here most sweetly'** *(Act 2 Scene 1, line 42)*. Fens are mentioned by Caliban twice, **'unwholesome fen'** *(Act 1 Scene 2, line 323)* and **'bogs, fens, flats'** *(Act 2 Scene 2, line 2)* and Antonio says, **'Or, as 'twere perfumed by a fen'** *(Act 2 Scene 1, line 51)*.

- Strachey writes at some length concerning discontent and conspiracy among the colonists on Bermuda, thus connecting, as Shakespeare did, the storm at sea with the storm of insurrection on land. Strachey writes, 'Yet there was a worse practise, faction and conjuration a foot, deadly and bloudy, in which the life of our Governour, and many others, were threatened'.

- Strachey makes reference to a book concerning the history of the islands of the West Indies and names the author as Gonzalus Ferdinandus Oviedus, which seems a likely source for the names Gonzalo and Ferdinand in the play.

For further discussion of correspondences between Strachey and Shakespeare see *Dating The Tempest* by David Kathman at
www.shakespeareauthorship.com/tempest.html.

Virgil's Aeneid: another love story

The story of the adventures of Aeneas would have been well known to many of Shakespeare's audience since the classics would have been taught to every schoolboy. Some may have recognised a number of the specific references to Virgil in the play, such as Ferdinand's **'Most sure the goddess'** *(Act 1 Scene 2, line 424)*, which echoes Virgil's 'O dea certe', or the sight of Ariel disguised **'like a harpy'** *(Act 3 Scene 3)*, the mythical bird that twice accosted Aeneas and his men.

The main reference in the play to the *Aeneid* comes in Act 2 Scene 1, lines 60–104, when Gonzalo compares Claribel, the new Queen of Tunis, with Dido, the former Queen of Carthage. The *Aeneid* tells of the journey made by Aeneas from Troy to Carthage, where he meets Dido. Under the instruction of the gods to continue his destiny, which was to be the founding of Rome, he leaves Dido, who, in despair, destroys herself.

There are some other parallels with *The Tempest*. Ferdinand's Mediterranean voyage ends in shipwreck, as does Aeneas's voyage from Troy, and both men suffer loss and pain in the aftermath. Afterwards, Ferdinand meets Miranda as Aeneas meets Dido. There is a supernatural element in each of the stories: Venus, in the case of Aeneas and Dido and Prospero's magic in the case of Miranda and Ferdinand. Also, in both stories, the hero leaves for Italy, for a new world and a new kind of society; though Aeneas leaves alone and Ferdinand and Miranda leave together. The general theme of humans being buffeted by nature and by supernatural powers is common to both stories.

Ovid's Metamorphoses: Shakespeare's elves

Ovid's *Metamorphoses* would also have been well known to many of Shakespeare's audience, either in the original Latin or in translation. Shakespeare probably used a popular translation by Arthur Golding, which was published in 1567.

In *Metamorphoses* Book VII, lines 197–209, Medea, the Greek goddess and magician, is calling upon her spirits:

> 'Ye Ayres and windes: ye Elves of Hilles, of Brookes, of Woods alone,
> Of standing Lakes, and of the Night approche ye everychone.
> Through helpe of whom (the crooked bankes much wondring at the thing)
> I have compelled streames to run cleane backward to their spring.
> By charmes I make the calme Seas rough, and make the rough seas plain
> And cover all the Skie with Cloudes, and chase them thence againe.
> By charmes I rayse and lay the windes, and burst the Vipers jaw,
> And from the bowels of the Earth both stones and trees doe drawe.
> Whole woods and Forestes I remove: I make the Mountaines shake,
> And even the Earth it selfe to grone and fearfully to quake.
> I call up dead men from their graves: and thee O lightsome Moone
> I darken oft, though beaten brasse abate thy perill soone.
> Our Sorcerie dimmes the Morning faire, and darkes the Sun at Noone.'

You can see how much Shakespeare used this source by comparing it to Prospero's speech in Act 5 Scene 1, lines 33–57.

Ovid's *Metamorphoses* is a long poem of fifteen books. It is a collection of legendary and mythological stories in which metamorphosis, or change, takes place. In this way it has a thematic connection with *The Tempest* since, in the play, most of the characters undergo some kind of change.

The characters and stories referred to in the masque in Act 4 are also found in Ovid's *Metamorphoses* and would have been widely known to Shakespeare's audience.

Shakespeare made use of his knowledge of history, literature and the classics in many of his plays. His use of the Strachey account, which had been recent news, and the popular and well-known stories of Virgil and Ovid would have made *The Tempest* immediately accessible and enjoyable to his audience.

The Tempest and the masque

A popular entertainment

The masque was a courtly entertainment, particularly lavish and splendid, with the players dressed up in costume and disguised with face masks and other adornments, often of a most elaborate kind. A typical masque might consist of a band of masquers who would arrive at some festivity, party or other social gathering, mingle and dance with the guests, offer gifts to the hosts and perform

With Inigo Jones as designer, the masque reached its high point.

some entertainment, pageant or drama. The masque might just be a procession and dancing, or it might be an elaborately staged show of drama, music and dance where, at some point, the masquers would descend from the staged performance, engage the guests in conversation, dancing or other revelry before returning to their pageant for farewell speeches and song. The subject of the performance usually came from Greek or Roman myths, or was allegorical and was presented to symbolise something relevant either to the host or the social gathering.

- In *The Tempest*, the masque in Act 4 Scene 1 celebrates the betrothal of Ferdinand and Miranda. It draws upon classical myth and symbolises peace and fertility. Iris, the goddess of the rainbow, signifies that the storm – the tempest and the political storm – is over; Ceres, goddess of the earth and agriculture, symbolises fertility and growth.

The masque probably had its roots in religious and folk ceremonies but soon became popular all over Europe. In Italy, under the patronage of Lorenzo de Medici, the masque became famous for its song, dance, elaborate scenery and sophisticated stage machinery. During the 16th century the European continental masque arrived in England, where it became a court entertainment enjoyed by Queen Elizabeth. These were sumptuous performances intended to amuse and compliment the Queen. During the reigns of the Stuart kings, with Ben Jonson as poet laureate and Inigo Jones his designer, the masque reached its high point. Under Jones's direction, masques were complex events that included all the art forms – painting, music, architecture and dance – as well as sophisticated mechanics. They were staged at great expense for weddings, birthdays and investitures. During the early part of this period, 1605 to 1634, Shakespeare would have been well aware of, and possibly part of, these extravaganzas. He wrote *The Tempest* after 1610 and there is a view that he may have added the masque later.

- There is a record of *The Tempest* being presented at Court in 1611 and then again during the winter of 1612–13, as part of the entertainments that were being enjoyed to celebrate the betrothal of King James I's daughter Elizabeth to Frederick V, Elector Palatine. Some people think that the original text had the masque added for either the betrothal celebrations or the wedding.

Jonson's *The Masque of Queens*, presented to King James I at Whitehall in 1609, included a prologue of grotesque witches who danced to 'hollow and infernal music'. This was the 'anti-masque' and it set off the true masquing dance of the 'Twelve Queenes-all' courtly ladies that followed.

Another of Jonson's masques, *Hymenaei*, performed for the wedding of the Earl of Essex and Lady Francis Howard in 1606, included Juno and Iris, as did Shakespeare's masque. The extravagance, richness of costume and lavishness of the Court masque did not make for a quiet, sober event. This is in contrast to Shakespeare's play, where Miranda's chastity and innocence are central to Prospero's purpose and Shakespeare's theme. Venus's and Cupid's desire to instil **'wanton charms'** upon Ferdinand and Miranda have been thwarted and **'no**

5

bed-rights shall be paid' until after the wedding. There is no suggestion of misbehaviour in Prospero's masque.

* The masque proper appears in Act 4, but the idea of the masque can be seen to be ever-present in *The Tempest*. There are numerous moments of song, dance, tableau and spectacle with Prospero as director. In tone, also, the play is mythical in its references to elements to be found in Virgil and is courtly and moral. The first encounter between Ferdinand and Miranda, when she is requested to **'the fringed curtain of thine eye advance'** *(Act 1 Scene 2, line 411)*, and other references to theatrical elements and stagecraft suggest masque. The banquet in Act 3 Scene 3, with its music, strange shapes and dance-mime, contains definite elements of masque – for example, its sudden disappearance by a **'quaint device'**.

* Ariel's disguise as a harpy suggests the elaborate costume of the masque and the dressing-up in **'trash'** of Stephano and Trinculo and the figure of Caliban suggest anti-masque.

The masque declined after Jonson's time and by the Civil War and the emergence of Puritanism it was over. The legacy is great, however, in theatrical forms such as opera, ballet and pantomime.

Utopias

In the following speech, which has been extracted as a whole from the play, Gonzalo, having arrived on the island which seems to be both deserted and pleasant, muses on what he would do to turn it into an ideal state.

'Had I plantation of this isle, my lord – …
And were the king on't, what would I do? …
I' th' commonwealth I would by contraries
Execute all things; for no kind of traffic
Would I admit; no name of magistrate;
Letters should not be known; riches, poverty,
And use of service, none; contract, succession,
Bourn, bound of land, tilth, vineyard, none;
No use of metal, corn, or wine, or oil;
No occupation; all men idle, all;
And women too, but innocent and pure;
No sovereignty –
All things in common nature should produce
Without sweat or endeavour; treason, felony,
Sword, pike, knife, gun, or need of any engine,
Would I not have; but nature should bring forth,
Of its own kind, all foison, all abundance,
To feed my innocent people.' *(Act 2 Scene 1, lines 127–47)*

Brave new worlds ... or not

The word 'utopia' literally means 'nowhere' and comes from the Greek words *ou* = not and *topos* = place. There is a long tradition of utopian writing. In the *Republic*, written in the 4th century BC, Plato sets out what he considers to be the ideal social, educational, political and philosophical rules for a city-state. Thomas More's *Utopia*, written in 1516, was concerned with describing the 'highest state of the republic' with elements of pagan and communist doctrines and as being entirely governed by reason. Francis Bacon's *New Atlantis*, published in 1627, leaned towards science, and centuries of other contributions are to be found.

Some utopian writing is presented as satire, which ridicules the attempts of mankind to aspire to anything ideal. Jonathan Swift's *Gulliver's Travels* (1726) and Samuel Butler's *Erewhon* (1872), are examples of this. In the 20th century, when totalitarian regimes seemed to be claiming the utopian ideal, writers began to describe the opposite, *dystopian*, state as a warning. *Nineteen Eighty-Four* by George Orwell (1949) is an example of this, as is Aldous Huxley's *Brave New World* (1932), which takes Miranda's innocent and hopeful phrase from Act 5 of *The Tempest* as the title for its dystopian tract.

Gonzalo's utopia

Michel Eyquem, seigneur de Montaigne, was a French courtier, traveller and essayist. His *Essais* were published in 1580 and translated into English in 1603. The essays included *Of the Caniballes*, which was certainly known by Shakespeare. The similarities between Montaigne's observations, gleaned from conversations with a servant who had lived amongst the Tupinambas (a South American people), and Gonzalo's utopia are interesting to note.

Montaigne describes the land of the 'caniballes' as being of 'exceeding pleasant and temperate situation', rather as Gonzalo found the island. Montaigne describes the society like this:

> 'It is a nation, would I answere Plato, that hath no kinde of traffike, no knowledge of Letters, no intelligence of numbers, no name of magistrate, nor of politike superioritie; no use of service, of riches or of poverty; no contracts, no successions, no dividences, no occupation but idle; no respect of kindred, but common, no apparrell but naturall, no manuring of lands, no use of wine, corne, or mettle. The very words that import lying, falshood, treason, dissimulation, covetousnes, envie, detraction, and pardon, were never heard of amongst them. How dissonant would hee finde his imaginary common-wealth from this perfection?'

At the time of the writing and performing of *The Tempest* people were aware of the possibility of social, political and religious upheaval. The question of the ideal state – the best way to live and be ruled – was not a remote, abstract question, but a real one. Within 50 years of Shakespeare writing *The Tempest* the people of England would execute their king and set up the 'Commonwealth'. Shakespeare had a keen sense of history and understood the minds of the people for whom he wrote.

Colonialism

In 1488 the sea route around southern Africa was first discovered and, four years later, in 1492, America was reached by explorers who had crossed the Atlantic. By the year 1500, colonialism had begun. European nations such as England, France, Portugal and Spain discovered, explored, conquered and settled large areas of the world. The voyages of now-famous men such as Francis Drake, Christopher Columbus, Bartolomeu Diaz and John Cabot opened up the world for exploration, exploitation and trade in the century before Shakespeare was writing *The Tempest*. The exploits of these men and many others like them aroused the interest not only of kings, queens and governments but also of ordinary people. There is evidence that Bristol seamen reached Newfoundland in 1492 but it was John Cabot, the Italian explorer, who sailed from Bristol under patent from Henry VII of England in 1497, who claims the first recorded exploration. After Henry's death in 1509 the English lost interest in discovery until 1553 when Asia, Russia and Frobisher's Northwest Passage were opened up.

By the end of 1588, when Shakespeare was 24 years old, Francis Drake had sailed around the world and had defeated the Spanish Armada, a victory that helped to open the way for English colonisation of America. Initially, the English West Indies was of more economic importance than the mainland. Despite trouble given by the ferocious Carib inhabitants, between 1609 and 1632, Englishmen settled the Leeward Islands and the Bermudas. Virginia, on the mainland, was founded in 1607. We know that some of these events had a quite direct effect upon Shakespeare and his writing of *The Tempest*. Stories about the discovery of islands, of savage peoples tamed by English gentlemen and of the 'planting' (see below) of settlers were very much in the air around 1610.

- *The Tempest* is concerned with notions of colonialism. Prospero has taken over the island and gained control over its inhabitants by his superior knowledge and art. He then makes the inhabitants, Ariel and Caliban, work for him and soon arranges for the island to be populated with more Europeans. Two of these further confuse the savage, native Caliban, making him drunk. After a time Prospero and the other Europeans leave and return the island to its original state and ownership, though that has, by now, much changed. This is, in short, a classic colonial model and although Prospero does not exploit the island for its natural resources, he does exploit Ariel's nimbleness and Caliban's labour.

- Two further characteristics of colonialism are also found in the play. Natives were treated kindly and given trinkets, which often belied the true colonial intention of their guests. Furthermore, the language of the conqueror was imposed, which is why so much of the world speaks Spanish or English. Caliban says that when Prospero came to the island first, he 'stroked' him and 'made much' of him; and Miranda taught him her language.

In Shakespeare's time both Africa and Ireland were highly topical places when considering policies of English colonialism. But given the sources for the play and the American, New World overtones, there is a tendency to think of Caliban, the natural inhabitant of the island on which he was born, as an American Indian or as a native of the West Indies. Stephano remarks, **'Do you play tricks upon's with savages and men of Ind?'** *(Act 2 Scene 2, lines 51–2)*. In support of this, there were any number of accounts by colonists that described natives such as Caliban, the savage monster, as barbarous, lustful, ferocious and generally uncivilised. We also know that native Americans were susceptible to alcohol. Alternatively, we can find kindly descriptions, such as those in Montaigne's *Of The Caniballes*, or Captain Arthur Barlow's description of the natives of Roanoake Island as 'most gentle, loving and faithful' and these, too, tie in with aspects of Caliban's complex nature.

- The island upon which Caliban was born is seen by Gonzalo as a potential utopia. However, he expresses this in colonial terms from the first phrase: **'Had I plantation of this isle'** *(Act 2 Scene 1, line 127)*. The word 'plantation' means the introduction of settlers and was first used by the English in respect of the colonisation of Ireland and then later of the Americas. 'Planting' implies supplanting the original population and imposing authority. Gonzalo can only establish his perfect place by interfering with the natural state of things and people. Gonzalo's vision is contradictory because he wants to impose a 'utopia' on a natural place and people by colonial means. This would amount to a 'fall' or 'lapse' in the perfect harmony of the island that Caliban knew, and is exactly what happened when Prospero arrived. This 'fall' or 'lapse' may be seen as an act of, or the cause of, brutality. We can see this happening in the Bible story about the Garden of Eden, where Eve's falling for temptation destroyed the original utopia. It could be argued that Caliban was brutalised by colonialisation. He was happily existing close to, and with an inborn understanding of, the nature of his island when Prospero came along and subjected him to his will, taught him a foreign language and gave him Miranda to look at. Miranda was Caliban's forbidden fruit.

Colonialism, as a fact of history, was beginning to develop at the time Shakespeare was writing *The Tempest*. For the 400 years since then it has influenced political, social and anthropological thinking in a way which Shakespeare could not have imagined. His play, however, illuminates the implications of some of those early beginnings.

Magic in *The Tempest*

Magic is central to *The Tempest* since without it none of the events could happen. Indeed, it is Prospero's Art which ensures that his project goes forward and more, for if, he tells us, he had not been so rapt by his books and neglectful of state business Antonio's usurpation would not have been successful in the first place. *The Tempest* might be said to be entirely dependent upon magic in the sense that all of the characters are manipulated by it and there is no one free of its effect. In this sense the manipulator, in the form of Prospero, is all-powerful, literally omniscient. But this is a power, an Art developed and used for a specific purpose and project and Prospero is careful to give it up before he returns to the world of Naples and Milan.

The title page from the 1623 folio edition.

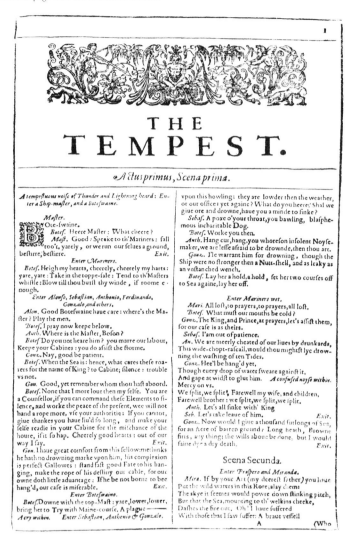

Shakespeare was writing during the time of James I, a monarch with strong views on magicians. James wrote in his *Daemonologie* that witches and magicians served 'both one Master, though in divers fashions' and that both deserved the punishment of death for doing so. Nor would Prospero's secret and all-consuming studies of his Art have met with James's approval, since James condemned those who, 'finding their practize to proove true in sundry things, they studie to know the cause thereof: and so mounting from degree to degree, upon the slippery and uncertaine scale of curiosity … to that black and unlawful science of magic'.

- In the play, Prospero is careful to distinguish his powers from those of Sycorax who practised an evil, retributive form of witchcraft that derived from the pagan god Setebos, and used toads, beetles and bats as familiars. Prospero is able to supersede this crude black magic by his refined Art and does so in releasing Ariel from the agony of the split pine. He also refers, in some of his later speeches, to the terminology associated with alchemy which, as a pseudo-scientific pursuit, was considered by many to belong more to studies such as astrology than witchcraft. The play itself can be seen as alchemical in that Prospero attempts to change the natures of Caliban, Antonio, Sebastian and Alonso from something base to something more moral.

• In the end, however, Prospero concedes that white and black magic cannot be distinguished and that both must be rejected before he can return to the real world.

Despite the outspoken aversion of the monarch and the Anglican Church, the Jacobean audience would have been familiar with and interested in magic, magicians and alchemy. There was widespread belief in the occult powers and the significance of quite ordinary things such as wells and crossroads. The audience would have been ready to accept the accoutrements of Prospero's Art; his staff and magic robe and, more especially in an illiterate society, the emphasis placed on his books.

Shakespeare listed with other actors of his time.

The Workes of William Shakespeare,
containing all his Comedies, Histories, and
Tragedies: Truely set forth, according to their first
ORIGINALL

The Names of the Principall Actors
in all these Playes.

William Shakespeare.	Samuel Gilburne.
Richard Burbadge.	Robert Armin.
John Hemmings.	William Ostler.
Augustine Phillips.	Nathan Field.
William Kempt.	John Underwood.
Thomas Poope.	Nicholas Tooley.
George Bryan.	William Ecclestone.
Henry Condell.	Joseph Taylor.
William Slye.	Robert Benfield.
Richard Cowly.	Robert Goughe.
John Lowine.	Richard Robinson.
Samuell Crosse.	Iohn Shancke.
Alexander Cooke.	Iohn Rice.

11

The characters

ALONSO, King of Naples

SEBASTIAN, his brother

ANTONIO, the usurping Duke of Milan, brother of Prospero

FERDINAND, son of Alonso

GONZALO, an honest old Councillor

ADRIAN, courtier

FRANCISCO, courtier

Other courtiers in the service of Alonso and Antonio

TRINCULO, a jester
STEPHANO, a drunken butler } in the service of Alonso

Master of the royal ship

Boatswain

Mariners

PROSPERO, the true Duke of Milan, brother of Antonio

MIRANDA, his daughter

ARIEL, an airy spirit

CALIBAN, a savage and deformed slave

IRIS
CERES
JUNO } Spirits in the masque
Nymphs
Reapers

Spirits in the shapes of dogs and hounds

1:1

The ship is returning to Naples from Tunis, where the wedding of Alonso's daughter has taken place. A violent tempest blows up and the ship is wrecked amidst great confusion.

1 *Boatswain* the ship's officer in charge of sails, rigging and summoning men to duty

3 *Good* unlikely to mean 'good cheer', rather, 'good to see you here'. *yarely* quickly

5 *my hearts* my hearty, courageous men. *cheerly* cheerfully, with a good will. *Yare* be quick

6 *Tend … whistle* The crew were directed by blasts from the shipmaster's whistle. *Blow … wind* the Boatswain challenges the storm to blow itself out, or the clouds to burst their cheeks

6–7 *if / room enough* There is dangerously little room between the ship and the rocks.

8 *Play the men* act with spirit, be manly

14 *roarers* loud, violent waves

17 *Councillor* one with authority and one who gives good advice

18 *work … presence* make the present moment (presence) peaceful

19 *hand … more* we will not need to handle any more rope

23–6 *Methinks … advantage* The proverb 'He that is born to be hanged never will be drowned' here expresses the idea that the rope which will hang the boatswain on land is a greater guarantee of safety than is the ship's anchor cable.

28 *Down … topmast* lower the mainsail

28–9 *Bring … course* adjust the 'try-sail' to slow the ship down

30 *plague* one of the Boatswain's many curses

30–1 *they are louder … office* The passengers are making more noise than the storm or the noise of the sailors working.

Down with the topmast! Yare, lower, lower!

1:1   *A tempestuous noise of thunder and lightning heard.*
           Enter SHIP-MASTER *and* BOATSWAIN

MASTER   Boatswain!

BOATSWAIN Here, Master. What cheer?

MASTER   Good. Speak to the mariners: fall to't yarely, or we run ourselves
           aground. Bestir, bestir.   [*Exit*

                           Enter MARINERS

BOATSWAIN Heigh, my hearts, cheerly, cheerly, my hearts. Yare, yare! Take in the   5
           topsail. Tend to the Master's whistle. Blow till thou burst thy wind, if
           room enough!

       Enter ALONSO, SEBASTIAN, ANTONIO, FERDINAND, GONZALO, *and* OTHERS

ALONSO   Good Boatswain, have care. Where's the Master? Play the men.

BOATSWAIN I pray now, keep below.

ANTONIO   Where is the Master, Boatswain?   10

BOATSWAIN Do you not hear him? You mar our labour; keep your cabins; you do
           assist the storm.

GONZALO   Nay, good be patient.

BOATSWAIN When the sea is. Hence, what cares these roarers for the name of
           King? To cabin – silence! Trouble us not.   15

GONZALO   Good, yet remember whom thou hast aboard.

BOATSWAIN None that I love more than myself. You are a Councillor; if you can
           command these elements to silence and work the peace of the presence,
           we will not hand a rope more. Use your authority: if you cannot, give
           thanks you have lived so long, and make yourself ready in your cabin for   20
           the mischance of the hour, if it so hap. Cheerly, good hearts! Out of our
           way, I say.   [*Exit*

GONZALO   I have great comfort from this fellow. Methinks he hath no drowning
           mark upon him, his complexion is perfect gallows. Stand fast, good
           Fate, to his hanging; make the rope of his destiny our cable, for our own   25
           doth little advantage; if he be not born to be hanged, our case is
           miserable.

       They all go out. The stage is empty for a moment; the storm increases in force.
                           Enter BOATSWAIN

BOATSWAIN Down with the topmast! Yare, lower, lower! Bring her to try with
           main course.

                          A cry off stage

           A plague upon this howling; they are louder than the weather, or our   30
           office.

34 *pox ... throat* may your throat be wracked by disease.
blasphemous The boatswain has been disrespectful towards his betters.

34–6 Notice how both Sebastian and Antonio use excessive cursing here and again in lines 45–8. What does this tell us about their characters?

38 *warrant him for* guarantee him from

39 *leaky ... wench* a woman whose menstrual bleeding is not stopped

40–1 *Lay ... off* hold the ship close to the wind then set the sails to drive the ship to the open sea

43 *cold* dead

45 *case* situation

46 *merely* wholly. *drunkards* Sailors had a reputation for drunkenness, especially when they thought they were going to drown.

47 *wide-chopped* big-mouthed

47–8 *lie ... tides* Courts of Admiralty sentenced pirates to be hanged on the shore at low-water mark and remain there until three tides had flowed and ebbed.

50 *glut* engulf

51 *we split* The ship is breaking up.

55 *furlongs* A furlong is an eighth of a mile.

56 *long heath* heather. *broom* a yellow-flowering shrub.
brown furze gorse

57 *fain* gladly

*The drama is heightened as the ship **splits**. How do the passengers react? What do the sailors do?*

Would the scene be played in darkness with lighting effects? How would this work?

What scenery and other constructions might there be on stage?

Make a note of your first impressions of Antonio, Sebastian and Gonzalo – their language and their attitude to other people and to the storm.

Look out for the development of these characters in Act 2 Scene 1 and see if your impressions are confirmed.

The ship is wrecked but near to land. The fate of the king, his courtiers and the sailors is unknown. The confused voices of the sailors – shouting farewell to their wives and children – suggest a watery death for all.

Enter SEBASTIAN, ANTONIO *and* GONZALO

Yet again? What do you here? Shall we give o'er and drown, have you a mind to sink?

SEBASTIAN   A pox o' your throat, you bawling, blasphemous, incharitable dog!

BOATSWAIN Work you then.   **35**

ANTONIO   Hang, cur, hang, you whoreson, insolent noisemaker: we are less afraid to be drowned than thou art.

GONZALO   I'll warrant him for drowning, though the ship were no stronger than a nutshell, and as leaky as an unstanched wench.

BOATSWAIN Lay her a-hold, a-hold! Set her two courses: off to sea again, lay her   **40** off.

Enter MARINERS, *wet*

MARINERS   All lost, to prayers, to prayers, all lost!

BOATSWAIN What, must our mouths be cold?

GONZALO   The King and Prince, at prayers – let's assist them,
For our case is as theirs.

SEBASTIAN   I'm out of patience.   **45**

ANTONIO   We are merely cheated of our lives by drunkards.
This wide-chopped rascal – would thou mightst lie drowning
The washing of ten tides!

GONZALO   He'll be hanged yet,
Though every drop of water swear against it,
And gape at wid'st to glut him.   **50**

VOICES [*Shouting confusedly from off stage*] Mercy on us! We split, we split!
Farewell, my wife and children! Farewell, brother! We split, we split, we split!

ANTONIO   Let's all sink with the King.

SEBASTIAN   Let's take leave of him.

[*Exeunt* ANTONIO *and* SEBASTIAN

GONZALO   Now would I give a thousand furlongs of sea for an acre of barren   **55**
ground: long heath, broom, furze, anything. The wills above be done,
but I would fain die a dry death.

[*Exeunt*

The Tempest

1:2

The inhabitants of the island – Prospero, Miranda, Ariel and Caliban – are introduced. Prospero's story is told and his authority demonstrated despite some murmurings of dissatisfaction.

1   *Art* magic

2   *allay them* calm them

3   *stinking pitch* the blackness of the clouds; pitch, or tar, was used in shipbuilding

4   *welkin's cheek* 'welkin' means sky or cloud; the shape of a cheek made by the clouds

5   *fire* lightning

6   *brave* splendid, magnificent

11   *or ere* before

13   *fraughting souls* cargo of souls; also the passengers were anxious because of the storm. *Be collected* calm yourself

14   *piteous* full of pity

16–21   Notice Prospero's repetition of 'thee', emphasising that Miranda is at the centre of his thoughts and of his plan.

18   Does the word 'Art', here, have more than one meaning?

19   *whence I am* where I came from

20   *poor cell* humble dwelling, usually represented as a cave on stage

21   *no greater* no more important than the humble home suggests; Prospero is in fact an usurped duke

22   *meddle … thoughts* cross my mind

25   *Lie … Art* Prospero addresses his magician's cloak

27   *virtue* essence

29   *safely ordered* properly arranged

30   *No … hair* 'Not a hair perished'. *perdition* loss

*Look at Miranda's speech on lines 1–13 and Prospero's reply to her. What do her words **dearest**, **brave**, **noble**, **poor**, **good**, tell us of her character?*

How would you want Miranda presented and played at this point if you were directing the scene?

31   *Betid* happened

35   *bootless inquisition* fruitless inquiry

1:2   *Enter* PROSPERO *and* MIRANDA

MIRANDA   If by your Art, my dearest father, you have
            Put the wild waters in this roar, allay them.
            The sky it seems would pour down stinking pitch,
            But that the sea, mounting to the welkin's cheek,
            Dashes the fire out. O, I have suffered   5
            With those that I saw suffer: a brave vessel,
            Who had no doubt some noble creature in her,
            Dashed all to pieces! O, the cry did knock
            Against my very heart. Poor souls, they perished.
            Had I been any god of power, I would   10
            Have sunk the sea within the earth, or ere
            It should the good ship so have swallowed, and
            The fraughting souls within her.

PROSPERO   Be collected;
            No more amazement. Tell your piteous heart
            There's no harm done.

MIRANDA   O woe the day!

PROSPERO   No harm.   15
            I have done nothing but in care of thee,
            Of thee my dear one, thee my daughter, who
            Art ignorant of what thou art, nought knowing
            Of whence I am, nor that I am more better
            Than Prospero, master of a full poor cell,   20
            And thy no greater father.

MIRANDA   More to know
            Did never meddle with my thoughts.

PROSPERO   'Tis time
            I should inform thee farther. Lend thy hand
            And pluck my magic garment from me. So,

                        Lays down his mantle

            Lie there my Art. Wipe thou thine eyes, have comfort.   25
            The direful spectacle of the wrack, which touched
            The very virtue of compassion in thee,
            I have with such provision in mine Art
            So safely ordered that there is no soul –
            No, not so much perdition as an hair,   30
            Betid to any creature in the vessel
            Which thou heard'st cry, which thou saw'st sink. Sit down,
            For thou must now know farther.

MIRANDA   You have often
            Begun to tell me what I am, but stopped
            And left me to a bootless inquisition,   35

19

41   *Out* quite

44   *Hath … remembrance* that you can remember

45   *assurance* certainty

46   *warrants* knows for sure

47   *tended* looked after

50   *dark backward* distant past. *abysm* abyss

56   *piece* masterpiece or model

59   *no worse issued* of no lesser birth than a princess

Prospero has often been represented as an old man. If he married young and Miranda, who is 15, is his only child, he could be younger. How old might Prospero be? What difference does this make to the way he might be acted?

This part of the scene is about private memories; how do the words on line 56 reflect this?

61   *blessèd* fortunate or an act of God

63   *holp* helped

64   *teen* trouble

65   *from* absent from

68–9   *he … loved* The importance of Antonio, next only to Miranda, suggests that Prospero's wife had died, possibly in childbirth.

69   *to him put* gave to him

70   *manage* management

71   *signories* the rulers of an Italian republic. *first* most important

Concluding, 'Stay, not yet'.

PROSPERO   The hour's now come.
    The very minute bids thee ope thine ear,
    Obey, and be attentive. Canst thou remember
    A time before we came unto this cell?
    I do not think thou canst, for then thou wast not   **40**
    Out three years old.

MIRANDA   Certainly, sir, I can.

PROSPERO   By what? by any other house, or person?
    Of any thing the image, tell me, that
    Hath kept with thy remembrance.

MIRANDA   'Tis far off,
    And rather like a dream than an assurance   **45**
    That my remembrance warrants: had I not
    Four or five women once, that tended me?

PROSPERO   Thou hadst, and more, Miranda. But how is it
    That this lives in thy mind? What seest thou else
    In the dark backward and abysm of time?   **50**
    If thou remember'st aught ere thou cam'st here,
    How thou cam'st here thou mayst.

MIRANDA   But that I do not.

PROSPERO   Twelve year since, Miranda, twelve year since,
    Thy father was the Duke of Milan and
    A prince of power.

MIRANDA   Sir, are not you my father?   **55**

PROSPERO   Thy mother was a piece of virtue, and
    She said thou wast my daughter; and thy father
    Was Duke of Milan, and his only heir
    A Princess, no worse issued.

MIRANDA   O the heavens,
    What foul play had we, that we came from thence?   **60**
    Or blessèd was't we did?

PROSPERO   Both, both, my girl.
    By foul play, as thou say'st, were we heaved thence,
    But blessedly holp hither.

MIRANDA   O my heart bleeds
    To think o' the teen that I have turned you to,
    Which is from my remembrance. Please you, farther.   **65**

PROSPERO   My brother and thy uncle, called Antonio –
    I pray thee mark me, that a brother should
    Be so perfidious – he, whom next thyself
    Of all the world I loved, and to him put
    The manage of my state, as at that time   **70**
    Through all the signories it was the first,

74	*those* the liberal arts
75–7	Prospero admits that he neglected his duties in favour of pursuing his study of magic.
76–7	*transported … studies* carried away with his studies of magic
78	*Dost … attend?* are you listening to me?
79	*suits* requests
81	*trash for over-topping* put down for being over-ambitious
82	*creatures* officials
82–3	*or … Or* either … or
83	*new formed* altered, changed
85	*that now he was* so that he became
86–7	*ivy … on't* an ivy-covered tree where each plant should nourish the other, but here the ivy extracted the tree's vitality
87	*verdure* strength, vitality
88	*mark me* pay attention

As he tells his story, Prospero's diction (manner of speaking) and syntax (the words he uses and the way he uses them) reflect his mood. Look at the dashes and the long, complicated sentences in lines 66–78. How would you describe his mood to an actor playing the part?

Read aloud Prospero's speech on lines 66–78 with movement and actions; try to bring out the mood as well as the meaning.

92	*O'er-prized … rate* the value of which was greater than most people thought
94	*beget* breed
97	*sans bound* without limit. *lorded* made like a lord with money and power
101	Antonio made his memory collude in his treachery.
103–4	*out o' the … royalty* by substituting his own position for Prospero's and playing the part of royalty
105	*prerogative* privilege of office
107	*no screen* No separation or division was possible between Antonio's role as duke and Prospero himself, so Antonio became the duke.
109	*Absolute* complete sovereign
110	*temporal royalties* secular, worldly powers
111	*confederates* makes alliance with
112	*dry* thirsty. *sway* power

And Prospero the prime duke, being so reputed
In dignity, and for the liberal arts
Without a parallel; those being all my study,
The government I cast upon my brother,   75
And to my state grew stranger, being transported
And rapt in secret studies. Thy false uncle –
Dost thou attend me?

MIRANDA   Sir, most heedfully.

PROSPERO   Being once pèrfected how to grant suits,
How to deny them, who t'advance, and who   80
To trash for over-topping, new created
The creatures that were mine, I say, or changed 'em,
Or else new formed 'em; having both the key
Of officer and office, set all hearts i' the state
To what tune pleased his ear, that now he was   85
The ivy which had hid my princely trunk,
And sucked my verdure out on't. Thou attend'st not?

MIRANDA   O good sir, I do.

PROSPERO   I pray thee mark me.
I thus neglecting worldly ends, all dedicated
To closeness and the bettering of my mind   90
With that which, but by being so retired,
O'er-prized all popular rate, in my false brother
Awaked an evil nature; and my trust,
Like a good parent, did beget of him
A falsehood in its contrary as great   95
As my trust was, which had indeed no limit,
A confidence sans bound. He being thus lorded,
Not only with what my revènue yielded,
But what my power might else exact, like one
Who having into truth, by telling of it,   100
Made such a sinner of his memory
To credit his own lie, he did believe
He was indeed the Duke, out o' the substitution
And executing th'outward face of royalty
With all prerogative. Hence his ambition growing –   105
Dost thou hear?

MIRANDA   Your tale, sir, would cure deafness.

PROSPERO   To have no screen between this part he played
And him he played it for, he needs will be
Absolute Milan. Me, poor man, my library
Was dukedom large enough. Of temporal royalties   110
He thinks me now incapable, confederates,
So dry he was for sway, wi' the King of Naples
To give him annual tribute, do him homage,

23

114–15	*Subject … crown* Antonio made Milan subject to Naples
117	*condition* the terms of agreement with Naples. *th'event* the outcome

Notice again the agitation indicated in the way Prospero is speaking on lines 89–106.

Find five or six angry and negative words in the speech.

How might Miranda say her line at 106? What might her less-than-noble thought about her grandmother be on lines 118–19?

123–4	in return for the obligations of their alliance and tribute paid
125	*presently extirpate* immediately wipe out
129	*Fated* destined
131	*ministers* those who carried out the deed, including Gonzalo
134	*hint* suggestion
135	*wrings mine eyes* makes me weep
137	*upon's* upon us
138	*impertinent* irrelevant. *Wherefore* why
139	*wench* young woman; a term of endearment
141–2	*set … bloody* physically harm us
144	*In few* briefly. *bark* small sailing boat
146	*carcass of a butt* rotten skeleton of a ship; like a cask or barrel
148	*have quit* had abandoned. *hoist* launched
151	*loving … wrong* the wind, though it blew the ship out to sea, pitied them

Subject his coronet to his crown and bend
The Dukedom yet unbowed – alas, poor Milan! –   115
To most ignoble stooping.

MIRANDA   O the heavens!

PROSPERO   Mark his condition and th'event, then tell me
If this might be a brother.

MIRANDA   I should sin
To think but nobly of my grandmother;
Good wombs have borne bad sons.

PROSPERO   Now the condition.   120
This King of Naples, being an enemy
To me inveterate, hearkens my brother's suit,
Which was that he, in lieu o' the premises
Of homage, and I know not how much tribute,
Should presently extìrpate me and mine   125
Out of the Dukedom, and confer fair Milan
With all the honours on my brother. Whereon,
A treacherous army levied, one midnight
Fated to the purpose, did Antonio open
The gates of Milan, and i' the dead of darkness   130
The ministers for the purpose hurried thence
Me, and thy crying self.

MIRANDA   Alack, for pity!
I, not remembering how I cried out then,
Will cry it o'er again. It is a hint
That wrings mine eyes to 't.

PROSPERO   Hear a little further,   135
And then I'll bring thee to the present business
Which now's upon's, without the which this story
Were most impertinent.

MIRANDA   Wherefore did they not
That hour destroy us?

PROSPERO   Well demanded, wench:
My tale provokes that question. Dear, they durst not,   140
So dear the love my people bore me; nor set
A mark so bloody on the business; but
With colours fairer painted their foul ends.
In few, they hurried us aboard a bark,
Bore us some leagues to sea, where they prepared   145
A rotten carcass of a butt, not rigged,
Nor tackle, sail nor mast – the very rats
Instinctively have quit it. There they hoist us,
To cry to the sea, that roared to us; to sigh
To the winds, whose pity sighing back again   150
Did us but loving wrong.

152	*cherubin*	cherub, angel
153	*preserve*	save
155	*decked*	adorned, covered with; also implies the deck of a boat
156	*which*	refers back to Miranda's smile
157	*undergoing stomach*	inner strength, determination
158	*what*	whatever
164	*stuffs*	stores and equipment
165	*steaded much*	been very useful. *gentleness* kindness
167	*volumes*	books on magic and liberal arts
168–9	*Would … man*	I wish that one day I might meet that man
169	*Now I arise*	Now I get up; an implied stage direction
170	*Sit still*	remain seated. *last* last part
172	*made thee more profit*	provided a more valuable education
174	*vainer hours*	leisure time
176	*beating in*	exercising
177	*Know thus far forth*	know this much
180	*prescience*	foreknowledge
181	*zenith*	the highest point of Fortune's wheel acting in Prospero's interest
182	*auspicious star*	lucky star, which should not be ignored. *influence* power
183	*omit*	ignore, disregard
185	*dulness*	sleepiness
186	*give it way*	give way to it, succumb

Prospero is much more positive and is warmer towards Miranda and about Gonzalo. Find and list some positive and uplifting words and phrases which would need to be emphasised on stage: for example, **cherubin**, **preserve**.

187	*Come away*	come here

26

MIRANDA   Alack, what trouble
      Was I then to you?

PROSPERO   O, a cherubin
      Thou wast that did preserve me. Thou didst smile,
      Infusèd with a fortitude from heaven,
      When I have decked the sea with drops full salt,   155
      Under my burden groaned; which raised in me
      An undergoing stomach, to bear up
      Against what should ensue.

MIRANDA   How came we ashore?

PROSPERO   By Providence divine.
      Some food we had, and some fresh water, that   160
      A noble Neapolitan, Gonzalo,
      Out of his charity – who being then appointed
      Master of this design – did give us, with
      Rich garments, linens, stuffs and necessaries
      Which since have steaded much; so, of his gentleness,   165
      Knowing I loved my books, he furnished me
      From mine own library with volumes that
      I prize above my Dukedom.

MIRANDA   Would I might
      But ever see that man!

PROSPERO   Now I arise,
      Sit still, and hear the last of our sea-sorrow.   170
      Here in this island we arrived, and here
      Have I, thy schoolmaster, made thee more profit
      Than other princes can, that have more time
      For vainer hours, and tutors not so careful.

MIRANDA   Heaven thank you for't. And now I pray you, sir,   175
      For still 'tis beating in my mind, your reason
      For raising this sea-storm?

PROSPERO   Know thus far forth:
      By accident most strange, bountiful Fortune
      (Now my dear Lady) hath mine enemies
      Brought to this shore; and by my prescience   180
      I find my zenith doth depend upon
      A most auspicious star, whose influence
      If now I court not, but omit, my fortunes
      Will ever after droop. Here cease more questions,
      Thou art inclined to sleep; 'tis a good dulness,   185
      And give it way; I know thou canst not choose.

                          MIRANDA *falls asleep*

      Come away, servant, come. I am ready now,
      Approach my Ariel. Come.   [*Enter* ARIEL

                                    27

190–2 Ariel describes some of the tasks he has done for Prospero's pleasure. Which elements is Ariel here associated with? What does this tell us about him?

192 *task* set tasks for

193 *quality* ability or helpers

194 *to point* to the smallest detail

195 *article* item

196 *beak* bow

197 *waist* middle of the ship

198 *flamed amazement* caused bewilderment by appearing as a flame

200 *yards, boresprit* the crossbars on the mast, the pole extending from the bow

201 *Jove's lightning* flashes of light associated with punishment or vengeance

203 *sight out-running* moved faster than could be seen

204 *sulphurous* associated with gunpowder and explosions

206 *dread trident* Neptune's three-pronged spear. *brave* fine

207 *coil* confusion

209 *of the mad* of the kind felt by mad people

209–10 *played … desperation* performed actions of despair

Ariel is a light, airy, quick spirit and there is a lot of movement indicated in his speech on lines 195–206. Explain or show how you would direct this scene using movement and space – leaping from rock to rock, using a stage hoist, scaffolding, flying wire.

How might a modern production use back-projection?

213 *up-staring* standing on end but probably not on fire

218 *sustaining garments* their garments supported them by holding them up in the water

220 *troops* groups

223 *angle* corner

224 *arms … knot* his arms folded across his chest

ARIEL   All hail, great master, grave sir, hail! I come
To answer thy best pleasure; be't to fly,   190
To swim, to dive into the fire, to ride
On the curled clouds; to thy strong bidding task
Ariel and all his quality.

PROSPERO   Hast thou, spirit,
Performed to point the tempest that I bade thee?

ARIEL   To every article.   195
I boarded the King's ship; now on the beak,
Now in the waist, the deck, in every cabin,
I flamed amazement; sometime I'd divide
And burn in many places; on the topmast,
The yards and boresprit would I flame distinctly,   200
Then meet, and join. Jove's lightning, the precursors
O' the dreadful thunder-claps, more momentary
And sight-outrunning were not; the fire and cracks
Of sulphurous roaring the most mighty Neptune
Seem to besiege, and make his bold waves tremble, 205
Yea, his dread trident shake.

PROSPERO   My brave spirit,
Who was so firm, so constant, that this coil
Would not infect his reason?

ARIEL   Not a soul
But felt a fever of the mad, and played
Some tricks of desperation; all but mariners   210
Plunged in the foaming brine, and quit the vessel,
Then all afire with me. The King's son Ferdinand,
With hair up-staring then, like reeds, not hair,
Was the first man that leaped; cried, 'Hell is empty,
And all the devils are here.'

PROSPERO   Why, that's my spirit!   215
But was not this nigh shore?

ARIEL   Close by, my master.

PROSPERO   But are they, Ariel, safe?

ARIEL   Not a hair perished:
On their sustaining garments not a blemish,
But fresher than before; and, as thou bad'st me,
In troops I have dispersed them 'bout the isle.   220
The King's son have I landed by himself,
Whom I left cooling of the air with sighs,
In an odd angle of the isle, and sitting,
His arms in this sad knot.

PROSPERO   Of the King's ship,
The mariners, say how thou hast disposed,   225
And all the rest o' the fleet.

228 *dew* an ingredient for a magical potion

229 *still-vexed Bermoothes* the Bermuda islands battered by ferocious storms (see page 1)

230 *stowed* confined safely

231 *suffered labour* hard work during the storm

234 *flote* afloat or the actual waves or sea

239 *mid season* noon

240 *two glasses* two hour glasses, ie at least 2 pm

241 *preciously* valuably

242 *pains* tasks to perform

243 *remember* remind. This is a reference to the proverb 'Great promise, small performance'.

244 *Moody* bad-tempered; Ariel is in a hurry to be freed

246 *time* agreed, or indentured time. Ariel's service to Prospero is based on a contract, as an apprentice would be to a master.

250 *bate* reduce – his indentured time

252 *think'st it much* you think it is too much to ask.
ooze the sludge on the ocean floor

255–6 *To do me … frost* to work for me in the hard frozen courses of the earth

255 *veins* the underground streams

256 *baked* hardened

258 *envy* malice

259 *hoop* bent over double

ARIEL   Safely in harbour
          Is the King's ship, in the deep nook where once
          Thou call'dst me up at midnight to fetch dew
          From the still-vexed Bermoothes – there she's hid;
          The mariners all under hatches stowed,   230
          Who, with a charm joined to their suffered labour,
          I have left asleep. And, for the rest o' the fleet,
          Which I dispersed, they all have met again
          And are upon the Mediterranean flote
          Bound sadly home for Naples,   235
          Supposing that they saw the King's ship wracked
          And his great person perish.

PROSPERO   Ariel, thy charge
          Exactly is performed; but there's more work.
          What is the time o' the day?

ARIEL   Past the mid season.

PROSPERO   At least two glasses. The time 'twixt six and now   240
          Must by us both be spent most preciously.

ARIEL   Is there more toil? Since thou dost give me pains,
          Let me remember thee what thou hast promised
          Which is not yet performed me.

PROSPERO   How now? Moody?
          What is't thou canst demand?

ARIEL   My liberty.   245

PROSPERO   Before the time be out? No more!

ARIEL   I prithee,
          Remember I have done thee worthy service,
          Told thee no lies, made no mistakings, served
          Without or grudge or grumblings; thou didst promise
          To bate me a full year.

PROSPERO   Dost thou forget   250
          From what a torment I did free thee?

ARIEL   No.

PROSPERO   Thou dost; and think'st it much to tread the ooze
          Of the salt deep,
          To run upon the sharp wind of the north,
          To do me business in the veins o' th' earth   255
          When it is baked with frost.

ARIEL   I do not, sir.

PROSPERO   Thou liest, malignant thing. Hast thou forgot
          The foul witch Sycorax, who with age and envy
          Was grown into a hoop? Hast thou forgot her?

ARIEL   No, sir.   260

266	*Argier*	Algeria
267–8	*for one thing … life*	Witches were executed unless they were pregnant. Sycorax was pregnant with Caliban.
270	*blue-eyed*	a bluish hue to the eyelids was thought to be a sign of pregnancy
273	*for*	because. *delicate* sensitive in nature
275	*hests*	behests, commands
276	*potent ministers*	powerful helpers
277	*unmitigable rage*	an anger which could not be calmed
278	*cloven pine*	a split in a pine tree
281	*vent thy groans*	cry out in pain
282	*mill-wheels strike*	as often as each blade of a mill wheel hits the water
283	*litter*	give birth to
284	*whelp*	the young of a dog
286	*Dull*	dark or lacking in intelligence – this seems to refer to Caliban
287	*in service*	as a servant. Prospero sees Caliban as a servant or slave, Ariel as an apprentice.
289	*penetrate the breasts*	arouse sympathy from
291–2	*Sycorax … undo*	Sycorax's inferior magical power could not reverse the spell.
293	*made gape*	opened up
296	*peg … entrails*	nail you in the tree's gnarled roots
298	*correspondent*	responsive
299	*gently*	without complaining

Notice that in describing Ariel's past life on the island and in threatening him, Prospero uses vivid, often short and violent words. Find some of these words between lines 270 and 297, words such as **hag** and **slave**.

How would you tell the actor playing Ariel to perform here?

PROSPERO   Thou hast: where was she born? Speak; tell me.

ARIEL   Sir, in Argier.

PROSPERO   O, was she so? I must
            Once in a month recount what thou hast been,
            Which thou forget'st. This damned witch Sycorax,
            For mischiefs manifold and sorceries terrible   265
            To enter human hearing, from Argier
            Thou know'st was banished – for one thing she did
            They would not take her life. Is not this true?

ARIEL   Ay, sir.

PROSPERO   This blue-eyed hag was hither brought with child,   270
            And here was left by the sailors. Thou, my slave,
            As thou report'st thyself, was then her servant;
            And, for thou wast a spirit too delicate
            To act her earthy and abhorred commands,
            Refusing her grand hests, she did confine thee   275
            By help of her more potent ministers,
            And in her most unmitigable rage,
            Into a cloven pine, within which rift
            Imprisoned, thou didst painfully remain
            A dozen years; within which space she died,   280
            And left thee there, where thou didst vent thy groans
            As fast as mill-wheels strike. Then was this island
            (Save for the son that she did litter here,
            A freckled whelp, hag-born) not honoured with
            A human shape.

ARIEL   Yes: Caliban her son.   285

PROSPERO   Dull thing, I say so – he, that Caliban
            Whom now I keep in service. Thou best know'st
            What torment I did find thee in; thy groans
            Did make wolves howl, and penetrate the breasts
            Of ever-angry bears; it was a torment   290
            To lay upon the damned, which Sycorax
            Could not again undo. It was mine Art,
            When I arrived, and heard thee, that made gape
            The pine, and let thee out.

ARIEL   I thank thee, master.

PROSPERO   If thou more murmur'st, I will rend an oak   295
            And peg thee in his knotty entrails till
            Thou hast howled away twelve winters.

ARIEL   Pardon, master;
            I will be correspondent to command
            And do my spriting gently.

PROSPERO   Do so; and after two days
            I will discharge thee.

301 *shall* must

304 *this shape* a robe or garment which, when worn, assures the audience of Ariel's invisibility

308 *Heaviness* sleepiness

310 *villain* the original sense of a low-born person or servant

312 *miss* do without

313 *in offices* duties

315 *Thou earth* Prospero emphasises the earthiness of Caliban in contrast to the airiness of Ariel. He is the fourth of the elements.

317 *tortoise. When?* a tortoise is slow, hence when will he arrive?

S.D. Ariel, though appearing as a water-nymph, is invisible

318 *fine* delicate and exquisite. *quaint* clever

320 *got* begotten; Caliban was fathered by the devil

321 *dam* mother

322 *wicked dew* an ingredient in black magic

323 *raven's feather* a raven was a familiar for witches.
fen bog or marsh

324 *South-west* Wind from the south-west was moist, warm and considered to be unhealthy.

325 *blister* cause infectious sores

327 *Side-stitches* pains in the side. *pen … up* stop your breath.
urchins an ancient word for hedgehogs

328 *for that … night* throughout the length of the night when evil spirits work

329 *exercise* practise

329–30 *pinched … honeycomb* pinched as densely as the cells in a honeycomb, which are formed by the bees pinching them into shape

330 *thick* frequent

ARIEL   That's my noble master!   300
    What shall I do? say what? what shall I do?

PROSPERO   Go make thyself like a nymph o' the sea, be subject to
    No sight but thine and mine: invisible
    To every eyeball else. Go take this shape
    And hither come in't; go: hence with diligence.   [*Exit* ARIEL   305
    [*To* MIRANDA] Awake, dear heart, awake, thou hast slept well.
    Awake.

MIRANDA   The strangeness of your story put
    Heaviness in me.

PROSPERO   Shake it off. Come on,
    We'll visit Caliban, my slave, who never
    Yields us kind answer.

MIRANDA   'Tis a villain, sir,   310
    I do not love to look on.

PROSPERO   But, as 'tis,
    We cannot miss him: he does make our fire,
    Fetch in our wood, and serves in offices
    That profit us. What ho! slave! Caliban!
    Thou earth, thou! speak.

CALIBAN [*Off-stage*]   There's wood enough within.   315

PROSPERO   Come forth, I say, there's other business for thee.
    Come, thou tortoise. When?

Enter ARIEL *like a water-nymph*

    Fine apparition! My quaint Ariel,
    Hark in thine ear.   [*Whispers to* ARIEL

ARIEL   My lord, it shall be done.   [*Exit*

PROSPERO   Thou poisonous slave, got by the devil himself   320
    Upon thy wicked dam, come forth.

Enter CALIBAN

CALIBAN   As wicked dew as e'er my mother brushed
    With raven's feather from unwholesome fen
    Drop on you both; a South-west blow on ye,
    And blister you all o'er.   325

PROSPERO   For this, be sure tonight thou shalt have cramps,
    Side-stitches that shall pen thy breath up; urchins
    Shall, for that vast of night that they may work,
    All exercise on thee; thou shalt be pinched
    As thick as honeycomb, each pinch more stinging   330
    Than bees that made 'em.

CALIBAN   I must eat my dinner.

332 Caliban claims that he inherited the island from Sycorax, his mother.

335 *Water with berries* cedar berries or grapes and thus wine

336 *bigger ... less* the sun and the moon; a reference from the Book of Genesis in the Bible

338 *qualities* characteristics

340 *charms* spells

343 *sty me* keep me confined like a pig in a sty

346 *stripes* beatings. *move* influence

347 *humane* human

350 Caliban here cheerfully admits his attempt at violating Miranda.

353 *print* imprint – on the mind

356–9 Miranda claims to have given meaning to Caliban's brutish gabbling, which he himself could not understand. She took trouble to make him speak and taught him language.

358 *thy purposes* things you wanted to say

359 *thy vile race* creatures like you

362 *rock* This implies a cave.

363 *more ... prison* worse punishment than imprisonment

What does Miranda's speech on lines 352–63 tell us about her character?

The actress playing Miranda would have been listening to Prospero for most of this long scene. This is her chance to speak. What are the key words in her speech. How would you have her deliver them?

Is she frightened of Caliban? What might she do to him when speaking? Which language did Miranda teach Caliban?

365 *red plague* blood spots were a symptom of the plague

366 *learning* teaching. *Hag-seed* offspring of a hag

367 *thou'rt best* you are advised to

368 *answer other business* get on with your work

370 *rack* as in torture on the rack

371 *aches* pronounced 'aitches', with two syllables

This island's mine by Sycorax my mother,
Which thou tak'st from me. When thou camest first
Thou strok'dst me, and made much of me; wouldst give me
Water with berries in't, and teach me how   335
To name the bigger light and how the less,
That burn by day and night; and then I loved thee,
And showed thee all the qualities o' th' isle,
The fresh springs, brine-pits, barren place and fertile –
Cursed be I that I did so. All the charms   340
Of Sycorax, toads, beetles, bats, light on you;
For I am all the subjects that you have,
Which first was mine own king; and here you sty me
In this hard rock, whiles you do keep from me
The rest o' th' island.

PROSPERO   Thou most lying slave,   345
Whom stripes may move, not kindness! I have used thee –
Filth as thou art – with humane care, and lodged thee
In mine own cell, till thou didst seek to violate
The honour of my child.

CALIBAN   Oh ho, oh ho, would't had been done!   350
Thou didst prevent me, I had peopled else
This isle with Calibans.

MIRANDA   Abhorrèd slave,
Which any print of goodness wilt not take,
Being capable of all ill! I pitied thee,
Took pains to make thee speak, taught thee each hour   355
One thing or other. When thou didst not, savage,
Know thine own meaning, but wouldst gabble, like
A thing most brutish, I endowed thy purposes
With words that made them known; but thy vile race,
Though thou didst learn, had that in't which good natures   360
Could not abide to be with; therefore wast thou
Deservedly confined into this rock,
Who hadst deserved more than a prison.

CALIBAN   You taught me language, and my profit on't
Is, I know how to curse. The red plague rid you   365
For learning me your language!

PROSPERO   Hag-seed, hence!
Fetch us in fuel, and be quick, thou'rt best,
To answer other business. Shrug'st thou, malice?
If thou neglect'st, or dost unwillingly
What I command, I'll rack thee with old cramps,   370
Fill all thy bones with aches, make thee roar,
That beasts shall tremble at thy din.

374 *Setebos* a Patagonian god and therefore from the New World; here connected with Caliban's mother (dam)

375 *vassal* slave

S.D. *invisible* Ariel is visible to himself and Prospero only – see lines 302–4. *playing* Ariel is probably playing a lute.

376 *yellow sands* Suggested by Virgil's *Aeneid* (see pages 2–3).

379 *whist* silent, hushed; the dancers are to kiss the wild waves to silence

380 *featly* skilfully, elegantly

382 *burden* refrain

S.D. *Here and there off-stage* The refrain is sung, not in harmony and, perhaps, from different parts of the stage.

387 *Chanticleer cry* song of a rooster

390 *waits upon* attends

394 *passion* suffering

395 *air* tune

398 *fathom* the traditional nautical measure of depth; one fathom is 6 feet

401 *fade* decay

402 *suffer* undergo

Ariel sings an **air** (line 395) accompanied by a lute. Ariel is light and graceful – the opposite, in all ways, to Caliban. How would you use costume, lights and other effects to represent each of these characters on stage?

Lines 398–404: We have music for some of Ariel's songs but not this one. Try it as a rap with a drum beat.

408 *ditty … remember* this song commemorates

409 *no mortal business* a supernatural event

410 *owes* owns

38

CALIBAN   No, pray thee.
        [*Aside*] I must obey; his Art is of such power
        It would control my dam's god Setebos,
        And make a vassal of him.

PROSPERO   So, slave, hence.   [*Exit* CALIBAN 375

    Enter ARIEL, *invisible, playing and singing, followed by* FERDINAND. ARIEL *sings*

        Come unto these yellow sands,
           And then take hands.
        Curtsied when you have and kissed,
           The wild waves whist,
        Foot it featly here and there   380
        And sweet sprites bear
           The burden. Hark, hark!

VOICES   [*Here and there off-stage*] Bow-wow!

ARIEL   The watch-dogs bark.

VOICES   [*Off*] Bow-wow!   385

ARIEL   Hark, hark! I hear
        The strain of strutting Chanticleer cry –

VOICES   [*Off*]   Cock-a-diddle-dow!

FERDINAND Where should this music be? I' th' air, or th'earth?
        It sounds no more; and sure it waits upon   390
        Some god o' th' island. Sitting on a bank,
        Weeping again the king my father's wrack,
        This music crept by me upon the waters,
        Allaying both their fury and my passion
        With its sweet air: thence have I followed it,   395
        Or it hath drawn me rather, but 'tis gone.
        No, it begins again.

                 ARIEL *sings*

        Full fathom five thy father lies;
           Of his bones are coral made;
        Those are pearls that were his eyes;   400
           Nothing of him that doth fade
        But doth suffer a sea-change
           Into something rich and strange.
        Sea-nymphs hourly ring his knell.

VOICES   [*Off-stage*] Ding-dong.   405

ARIEL   Hark now I hear them.

VOICES   [*Off*] Ding-dong bell.

FERDINAND The ditty does remember my drowned father.
        This is no mortal business, nor no sound
        That the earth owes. I hear it now above me.   410

411	*fringèd … advance* eyelashes raised up
412	*yond* over there
414	*brave form* handsome shape. *But* alas
416	*gallant* fine gentleman
417	*but* except that. *something* somewhat
418	*canker* destroyer
419	*goodly* handsome

Various words are used to describe Ferdinand between lines 412 and 422 – find them in the text.

What do you think Ferdinand should look like?

*Miranda says that he **looks about**; what might he be actually doing?*

422	*It goes on* my plan is working
424	*Most … goddess* The words are from Virgil's *Aeneid* Book 1, lines 328–5 (see pages 2–3).
424–5	this is the goddess for whom these songs are sung
426	tell me if you live on this island
428	*bear me* conduct myself; behave
429	*wonder* Miranda's name means 'wonder', from the Latin, 'miror' – to wonder.
430	*maid* human, rather than a goddess, and unmarried. *My language* Ferdinand, a Neopolitan, is astonished to find that Miranda speaks his language.
432	*best* highest in rank
435	*single* one and the same person
436–7	*He does … weep* Ferdinand is saying that, since he is the King of Naples, he can hear himself but that this fact makes him weep for his father's death.
438	*never … ebb* which have not stopped crying
439	*for mercy* may God have mercy
441	*his brave son* The Duke of Milan's (Antonio's) son is never again mentioned in the play.
442	*control thee* rebuke you
444	*changed eyes* looked into each other's eyes; love at first sight

40

PROSPERO [*To* MIRANDA] The fringèd curtains of thine eye advance,	
And say what thou seest yond.	
MIRANDA What is't? a spirit?	
Lord, how it looks about. Believe me, sir,	
It carries a brave form. But 'tis a spirit.	
PROSPERO No, wench, it eats, and sleeps, and hath such senses	**415**
As we have – such. This gallant which thou seest	
Was in the wrack, and, but he's something stained	
With grief (that's beauty's canker), thou mightst call him	
A goodly person. He hath lost his fellows,	
And strays about to find 'em.	
MIRANDA I might call him	**420**
A thing divine, for nothing natural	
I ever saw so noble.	
PROSPERO [*Aside*] It goes on, I see,	
As my soul prompts it. Spirit, fine spirit, I'll free thee	
Within two days for this.	
FERDINAND Most sure the goddess	
On whom these airs attend! Vouchsafe my prayer	**425**
May know if you remain upon this island,	
And that you will some good instruction give	
How I may bear me here. My prime request,	
Which I do last pronounce, is – O you wonder –	
If you be maid, or no?	
MIRANDA No wonder, sir,	**430**
But certainly a maid.	
FERDINAND My language? Heavens!	
I am the best of them that speak this speech,	
Were I but where 'tis spoken.	
PROSPERO How? the best?	
What wert thou if the King of Naples heard thee?	
FERDINAND A single thing, as I am now, that wonders	**435**
To hear thee speak of Naples. He does hear me,	
And that he does, I weep. Myself am Naples,	
Who with mine eyes, never since at ebb, beheld	
The King my father wracked.	
MIRANDA Alack, for mercy.	
FERDINAND Yes, faith, and all his lords, the Duke of Milan	**440**
And his brave son being twain.	
PROSPERO [*Aside*] The Duke of Milan	
And his more braver daughter could control thee	
If now 'twere fit to do't. At the first sight	
They have changed eyes. Delicate Ariel,	
I'll set thee free for this. [*To* FERDINAND] A word, good sir,	**445**

446 *done … wrong* made an error

449 *Pity move* let compassion persuade

450–2 Ferdinand here offers to marry Miranda if she is not betrothed to anyone else and if she is a virgin.

452 *Soft* a call for silence

454–5 *lest … prize light* winning Miranda too easily might cheapen the conquest

455 *charge* command

456 *attend* pay attention to

457 *ow'st not* do not own

460–2 Miranda expresses the philosophical view that beauty of form and beauty of spirit are inseparable; if there is anything evil in a beautiful body then good will overcome it. Here is a further example of Miranda's capacity to express a viewpoint.

466 *fresh-brook mussels* These are inedible.

468 *entertainment* treatment

471 The line has two possible meanings: that Ferdinand is tame and not to be feared and that he is noble and not a coward.

471 *not fearful* not causing fear, ie mild

472 *My foot … tutor* From the proverb 'Do not make the foot the head'; Prospero will not be told what to do by his daughter

474 *Come, from* stop. *ward* defensive posture

475 *stick* Prospero's magic wand.

476 *weapon drop* a sexual innuendo; Prospero is suggesting that he has the power to disarm Ferdinand and reduce his manhood

477 *hang … garments* Miranda is trying to restrain Prospero.

478 *be his surety* stand up for him, be his guarantee

I fear you have done yourself some wrong; a word.

MIRANDA   [*Aside*] Why speaks my father so ungently? This
　　　　　　Is the third man that e'er I saw, the first
　　　　　　That e'er I sighed for. Pity move my father
　　　　　　To be inclined my way!

FERDINAND　　　　　　　　　　O, if a virgin,　　　　　　**450**
　　　　　　And your affection not gone forth, I'll make you
　　　　　　The Queen of Naples.

PROSPERO　　　　　　　　　Soft, sir, one word more.
　　　　　　[*Aside*] They are both in either's powers; but this swift business
　　　　　　I must uneasy make, lest too light winning
　　　　　　Make the prize light. [*To* FERDINAND] One word more. I charge thee　**455**
　　　　　　That thou attend me. Thou dost here usurp
　　　　　　The name thou ow'st not, and hast put thyself
　　　　　　Upon this island as a spy, to win it
　　　　　　From me, the lord on't.

FERDINAND　　　　　　　　No, as I am a man.

MIRANDA   There's nothing ill can dwell in such a temple;　**460**
　　　　　　If the ill spirit have so fair a house,
　　　　　　Good things will strive to dwell with't.

PROSPERO　　　　　　　　　　　　　Follow me.
　　　　　　[*To* MIRANDA] Speak not you for him; he's a traitor. [*To* FERDINAND] Come,
　　　　　　I'll manacle thy neck and feet together,
　　　　　　Sea-water shalt thou drink, thy food shall be　**465**
　　　　　　The fresh-brook mussels, withered roots, and husks
　　　　　　Wherein the acorn cradled. Follow.

FERDINAND　　　　　　　　　　No,
　　　　　　I will resist such entertainment, till
　　　　　　Mine enemy has more power.

He draws his sword, but PROSPERO'S *magic prevents him from moving*

MIRANDA　　　　　　　　　O dear father,
　　　　　　Make not too rash a trial of him, for　　　　**470**
　　　　　　He's gentle, and not fearful.

PROSPERO　　　　　　　　　What, I say,
　　　　　　My foot my tutor? Put thy sword up, traitor,
　　　　　　Who mak'st a show, but dar'st not strike, thy conscience
　　　　　　Is so possessed with guilt. Come, from thy ward,
　　　　　　For I can here disarm thee with this stick,　**475**
　　　　　　And make thy weapon drop.

MIRANDA　　　　　　　　　Beseech you, father.

PROSPERO   Hence, hang not on my garments.

MIRANDA　　　　　　　　　　Sir, have pity;
　　　　　　I'll be his surety.

43

The Tempest

481 *such shapes* human males

Where and in what different ways has Prospero used his power with Ferdinand and Miranda?

Who else has Prospero threatened and with what similar words?

*On line 479, Prospero says **chide thee** and **hate thee** to Miranda; how might she react to that?*

483	*To* compared to
487–8	*Thy ... in them* you are as weak as an infant
487	*nerves* sinews, strength
491	*wrack* death. *nor* and
492	*light* minor matters
493	*through* from
494	*all ... earth* anywhere else
495	*liberty* those who have liberty
498	*do me* do for me
500	*unwonted* unusual
501–2	*free ... winds* as free as air
502–3	*but ... command* If Ariel is to be as free as the wind he must do exactly as Prospero commands.

*What does **It works** on line 496 tell us about Prospero? Who might he be saying this to?*

*Miranda says to Ferdinand, **My father's of a better nature, sir, / Than he appears by speech.** Which modern saying does this remind you of?*

It has been quite an afternoon for Miranda, so far! Compare her state of mind, what she knew about herself and her emotional feelings at the beginning of Act 1 Scene 2 with what they are at the end.

Look out for the development of Caliban's character in Act 2 Scene 2. Make notes about your first impressions of him here in Act 1 Scene 2 – what he is and what he stands for. He has been called the 'core of the play'.

By the end of this long scene, Miranda has come to know the story of her removal from Milan and the treachery of Antonio and the others. The audience has met Ariel and Caliban, Prospero's two very different slaves, learned something about each of them and formed some opinions of them. Shakespeare has also sown the seeds of a romance between Ferdinand and Miranda.

44

PROSPERO   Silence! one word more
    Shall make me chide thee, if not hate thee. What,
    An advocate for an impostor? Hush!   480
    Thou think'st there is no more such shapes as he,
    Having seen but him and Caliban; foolish wench,
    To the most of men, this is a Caliban,
    And they to him are angels.

MIRANDA   My affections
    Are then most humble; I have no ambition   485
    To see a goodlier man.

PROSPERO   Come on, obey.
    Thy nerves are in their infancy again,
    And have no vigour in them.

FERDINAND   So they are.
    My spirits, as in a dream, are all bound up;
    My father's loss, the weakness which I feel,   490
    The wrack of all my friends, nor this man's threats
    To whom I am subdued, are but light to me,
    Might I but through my prison once a day
    Behold this maid: all corners else o' th' earth
    Let liberty make use of; space enough   495
    Have I in such a prison.

PROSPERO   [*Aside*]   It works. [*To* FERDINAND] Come on.
    [*To* ARIEL] Thou hast done well, fine Ariel. Follow me;
    Hark what thou else shalt do me.

MIRANDA   Be of comfort;
    My father's of a better nature, sir,
    Than he appears by speech. This is unwonted   500
    Which now came from him.

PROSPERO   [*To* ARIEL]   Thou shalt be as free
    As mountain winds; but then exactly do
    All points of my command.

ARIEL   To the syllable.

PROSPERO   [*To* FERDINAND] Come, follow. [*To* MIRANDA] Speak not for him.

                                                    [*Exeunt*

45

2:1

The king and his party have all survived the shipwreck and are scattered around the island. They reveal their different attitudes to the situation and their impressions of the island. A murder is plotted, and prevented by Ariel.

3   *beyond* greater than. *hint* occasion

5   *masters … the merchant* the officers of some merchant vessel and the owner. In a scene which thrives on puns, this could be an early example.

6   *theme* topic, subject

8   *weigh* balance

9–10 *peace … porridge* a pun on the rhyme 'pease-porridge hot, pease-porridge cold'

11   A 'visitor' is a person who visits a hospital or prison in order to bring comfort.

13   *strike* his wit and his watch will strike, striking watches were fashionable

15   *One. Tell.* Sebastian counts and invites Antonio to keep count.

16–19 Gonzalo says that sorrow comes to the 'entertainer' of every grief.

18   *dollar* payment for entertainment

19   *Dolour* sadness, sorrow. Gonzalo's pun is wittier than Sebastian's interruption.

20   *purposed* intended

24   *spare* stop, spare me

25   *talking* proverb; 'The greatest talkers are the least doers'

26–9 Antonio and Sebastian bet on who will be first to 'crow', Gonzalo, the 'old cock' or Adrian, the young 'cockerel'.

30   *A laughter* a pun: the word 'laughter' also means, 'the whole number of eggs laid by a fowl before she is ready to sit'

32   *desert* uninhabited

2:1   *Enter* ALONSO, SEBASTIAN, ANTONIO, GONZALO, ADRIAN, FRANCISCO,
and other COURTIERS

GONZALO	Beseech you, sir, be merry; you have cause
	(So have we all) of joy; for our escape
	Is much beyond our loss. Our hint of woe
	Is common; every day, some sailor's wife,
	The masters of some merchant, and the merchant

5

	Have just our theme of woe; but for the miracle –
	I mean our preservation – few in millions
	Can speak like us. Then wisely, good sir, weigh
	Our sorrow with our comfort.
ALONSO	Prithee, peace.
SEBASTIAN	[*Aside to* ANTONIO] He receives comfort like cold porridge.

10

ANTONIO	[*Aside to* SEBASTIAN] The visitor will not give him o'er so.
SEBASTIAN	[*Aside to* ANTONIO] Look, he's winding up the watch of his wit; by
	and by it will strike.
GONZALO	Sir –
SEBASTIAN	[*Aside to* ANTONIO] One. Tell.

15

GONZALO	When every grief is entertained that's offered,
	Comes to th'entertainer –
SEBASTIAN	A dollar.
GONZALO	Dolour comes to him indeed; you have spoken truer than you
	purposed.

20

SEBASTIAN	You have taken it wiselier than I meant you should.
GONZALO	Therefore, my Lord –
ANTONIO	Fie, what a spendthrift is he of his tongue.
ALONSO	I prithee, spare.
GONZALO	Well, I have done. But yet –
SEBASTIAN	He will be talking.

25

ANTONIO	Which, of he or Adrian, for a good wager, first begins to crow?
SEBASTIAN	The old cock.
ANTONIO	The cockerel.
SEBASTIAN	Done: the wager?
ANTONIO	A laughter.

30

SEBASTIAN	A match.
ADRIAN	Though this island seem to be desert –
ANTONIO	Ha, ha, ha!
SEBASTIAN	So, you're paid.
ADRIAN	Uninhabitable, and almost inaccessible –

35

38 *miss 't* Adrian could not miss the opportunity to talk

39 *subtle* refined

40 *Temperance* a pun: Antonio refers to the name for a woman, Adrian means the climate

41 *subtle* crafty or sexually clever. *learnedly delivered* spoken with authority

44 *fen* foul-smelling marshland

45 *advantageous* useful

48 *lush* luxuriant or soft and tender

49 *tawny* tan-coloured

50 *eye of green* tinge

53 *credit* belief

54 *vouched rarities* unusual events said to be true; another sarcastic remark

56 *glosses … new-dyed* Gonzalo observes that their clothes look brand new.

There are now at least six characters on stage, with Antonio and Sebastian together but close enough to interrupt and make fun of Gonzalo. How would you arrange the characters? What would your set design look like for this scene?

Gonzalo makes a remark about their clothes on lines 55–7. How would you have the characters dressed? Draw some costume designs.

58 *pockets* the insides of his pockets

59 *pocket up* conceal. Antonio's use of 'pockets' on line 58 sets up the pun here.

62 *Tunis* A city-state, as Carthage was earlier.

63 *prosper* In a scene that celebrates punning, Shakespeare could not resist this ironic one on Prospero's name.

64 *to* for

65 *widow Dido* Dido was the widow of Sychaeus. She killed herself when her lover, the widower Aeneas, abandoned her.

66–7 *Dido. Aeneas* In typical poor taste it is likely that Antonio and Sebastian are here punning on the names Dido – 'die, do' and Aeneas – 'any ass'.

69 *study of* think about

70 Carthage and Tunis were not, in fact, the same place.

74–5 *miraculous harp … houses too* Amphibion's harp raised only the walls of Thebes. Gonzalo would replace the whole of Carthage with Tunis.

SEBASTIAN	Yet –	
ADRIAN	Yet –	
ANTONIO	He could not miss 't.	
ADRIAN	It must needs be of subtle, tender, and delicate temperance.	
ANTONIO	Temperance was a delicate wench.	**40**
SEBASTIAN	Ay, and a subtle, as he most learnedly delivered.	
ADRIAN	The air breathes upon us here most sweetly.	
SEBASTIAN	As if it had lungs, and rotten ones.	
ANTONIO	Or as 'twere perfumed by a fen.	
GONZALO	Here is everything advantageous to life.	**45**
ANTONIO	True, save means to live.	
SEBASTIAN	Of that there's none, or little.	
GONZALO	How lush and lusty the grass looks! How green!	
ANTONIO	The ground indeed is tawny.	
SEBASTIAN	With an eye of green in 't.	**50**
ANTONIO	He misses not much.	
SEBASTIAN	No, he doth but mistake the truth totally.	
GONZALO	But the rarity of it is, which is indeed almost beyond credit –	
SEBASTIAN	As many vouched rarities are.	
GONZALO	That our garments, being – as they were – drenched in the sea, hold notwithstanding their freshness and glosses, being rather new-dyed than stained with salt water.	**55**
ANTONIO	If but one of his pockets could speak, would it not say he lies?	
SEBASTIAN	Ay, or very falsely pocket up his report.	
GONZALO	Methinks our garments are now as fresh as when we put them on first in Afric, at the marriage of the King's fair daughter Claribel to the King of Tunis.	**60**
SEBASTIAN	'Twas a sweet marriage, and we prosper well in our return.	
ADRIAN	Tunis was never graced before with such a paragon to their queen.	
GONZALO	Not since widow Dido's time.	**65**
ANTONIO	Widow? A pox o' that. How came that widow in? Widow Dido!	
SEBASTIAN	What if he had said 'widower Aeneas' too? Good Lord, how you take it!	
ADRIAN	'Widow Dido,' said you? You make me study of that; she was of Carthage, not of Tunis.	**70**
GONZALO	This Tunis, sir, was Carthage.	
ADRIAN	Carthage?	
GONZALO	I assure you, Carthage.	
ANTONIO	His word is more than the miraculous harp.	

76–9   In Shakespeare's play *Antony and Cleopatra*, Cleopatra says of Antony, 'realms and islands were / As plates dropped from his pocket'.

79   *kernels* seeds

81   *in good time* This may signal the timely reappearance in the text of Alonso, thus relieving Antonio of Gonzalo's talking.

85   *Bate* except for

87–8   *in a sort* in a way

89   *sort* kind, variety – thus making the pun

91–2   *You … sense* Alonso complains that he is being forced to hear their chattering against his will.

92   *sense* disposition, feelings

94   *rate* estimation, belief

97   *Naples … Milan* Alonso here states his intention that Ferdinand was to inherit the dukedom of Milan. What effect might this have on Antonio, who can hear what he is saying?

99–104   Similar to a passage in Virgil's *Aeneid* with serpents 'breasting the sea …'.

99   *beat the surges* push the waves down.

101   *enmity* opposition – the surging waves attacked him. *breasted* confronted with his chest

103–4   *oared / Himself* used his arms as oars

105   *wave-worn* eroded by waves. *basis* bottom of the cliff. *bowed* arched inward

106   *stooping* leaning over. *relieve* help

Francisco's only long speech, in blank verse, is particularly poetic. Read the speech aloud emphasising the diction and imagery.

Mark the words in the text which you will stress.

Is this a realistic account of what Francisco saw – or is his intention different?

108   *thank yourself* blame yourself

110   *loose* lose; or a pun on 'loose' in that she is now unchased

112   *wet … on't* weep for the sorrow of it

113   *importuned* harassed with requests

SEBASTIAN	He hath raised the wall, and houses too.	75
ANTONIO	What impossible matter will he make easy next?	
SEBASTIAN	I think he will carry this island home in his pocket, and give it his son for an apple.	
ANTONIO	And sowing the kernels of it in the sea, bring forth more islands.	
GONZALO	Ay.	80
ANTONIO	Why, in good time.	
GONZALO	Sir, we were talking, that our garments seem now as fresh as when we were at Tunis at the marriage of your daughter, who is now Queen.	
ANTONIO	And the rarest that e'er came there.	
SEBASTIAN	Bate, I beseech you, widow Dido.	85
ANTONIO	O, widow Dido! Ay, widow Dido.	
GONZALO	Is not, sir, my doublet as fresh as the first day I wore it? I mean in a sort.	
ANTONIO	That sort was well fished for.	
GONZALO	When I wore it at your daughter's marriage.	90

ALONSO   You cram these words into mine ears against
The stomach of my sense. Would I had never
Married my daughter there, for coming thence
My son is lost, and, in my rate, she too,
Who is so far from Italy removed,   95
I ne'er again shall see her. O thou mine heir
Of Naples and of Milan, what strange fish
Hath made his meal on thee?

FRANCISCO   Sir, he may live.
I saw him beat the surges under him,
And ride upon their backs; he trod the water,   100
Whose enmity he flung aside, and breasted
The surge most swoln that met him; his bold head
'Bove the contentious waves he kept, and oared
Himself with his good arms in lusty stroke
To the shore, that o'er his wave-worn basis bowed,   105
As stooping to relieve him. I not doubt
He came alive to land.

ALONSO   No, no, he's gone.

SEBASTIAN   Sir, you may thank yourself for this great loss,
That would not bless our Europe with your daughter,
But rather loose her to an African,   110
Where she, at least, is banished from your eye,
Who hath cause to wet the grief on't.

ALONSO   Prithee, peace.

SEBASTIAN   You were kneeled to and importuned otherwise

115 *Weighed* balanced. *loathness* hatred at the idea of marrying the king of Tunis. *obedience* to her father's arrangement of her marriage

116 *end ... bow* which way the scale should tip

118 *widows* of all the dead mariners

120 *dear'st* most loved, ie Ferdinand

122 *time* right time

123 *plaster* medical dressing

124 *chirurgeonly* like a surgeon, ie cuttingly

125 *foul* the mood of the king and another pun on fowl

127 *plantation* colonial settlement

128 *nettle-seed* a prickly weed. *docks* a coarse weedy herb and antidote for nettles. *mallows* a wild plant with hairy stems and reddish purple flowers

Sebastian and Antonio make fun of Gonzalo with their puns and repartee; they are also insensitive to Alonso's grief. Would you have them perform their lines
• *directly to the characters on stage?*
• *to each other only?*
• *as asides?*
• *with grand gestures to the audience?*

Choose some of these occasions and add stage directions for Sebastian and Antonio.

131 *commonwealth* a nation or self-governing community. *by contraries* different from normal customs

132 *traffic* business, commerce

133 *admit* allow

134 *letters* learning, intellectual pursuits

135 *use of service* employment of servants. *contract* written demands of employment. *succession* as in inheriting title or privilege

136 *Bourn ... bound* rigid boundaries of land. *tilth* farm labour

137 *use of metal* ie precious metal, money or possibly money-lending

138 *occupation* employment; also meant 'to cohabit'

138–9 *idle ... pure* unoccupied and chaste; a contradiction of the proverb 'Idleness begets lust'

140 *sovereignty* monarchy

141 *forgets* contradicts

142–3 *All ... endeavour* all men should share without exploitation

144 *engine* a machine of war

146 *Of its own kind* naturally. *foison* plenty

149 *idle* wanton, frivolous

	By all of us; and the fair soul herself	
	Weighed between loathness and obedience, at	115
	Which end o' the beam should bow. We have lost your son,	
	I fear for ever; Milan and Naples have	
	Mo widows in them of this business' making	
	Than we bring men to comfort them. The fault's your own.	

ALONSO   So is the dear'st o' the loss.

GONZALO   My lord Sebastian,   120
The truth you speak doth lack some gentleness,
And time to speak it in. You rub the sore
When you should bring the plaster.

SEBASTIAN   Very well.

ANTONIO   And most chirurgeonly.

GONZALO   It is foul weather in us all, good sir,   125
When you are cloudy.

SEBASTIAN   Fowl weather?

ANTONIO   Very foul.

GONZALO   Had I plantation of this isle, my lord –

ANTONIO   He'd sow 't with nettle-seed.

SEBASTIAN   Or docks, or mallows.

GONZALO   And were the king on't, what would I do?

SEBASTIAN   'Scape being drunk, for want of wine.   130

GONZALO   I' the commonwealth I would by contraries
Execute all things; for no kind of traffic
Would I admit; no name of magistrate;
Letters should not be known; riches, poverty,
And use of service, none; contract, succession,   135
Bourn, bound of land, tilth, vineyard, none;
No use of metal, corn, or wine, or oil;
No occupation, all men idle, all;
And women too, but innocent and pure;
No sovereignty –

SEBASTIAN   Yet he would be king on't.   140

ANTONIO   The latter end of his commonwealth forgets the beginning.

GONZALO   All things in common Nature should produce
Without sweat or endeavour; treason, felony,
Sword, pike, knife, gun, or need of any engine
Would I not have; but Nature should bring forth   145
Of it own kind all foison, all abundance,
To feed my innocent people.

SEBASTIAN   No marrying 'mong his subjects?

ANTONIO   None, man, all idle; whores and knaves.

151   *Golden Age*   from Ovid; before man's fall, before man lapsed into wickedness.   *'Save*   God save

152   *mark*   take notice of

154   *minister occasion*   create an opportunity (to amuse)

155   *sensible and nimble*   sensitive and quick

156   *nothing*   wordplay on the meaning of no physical thing and of no importance

160   *blow*   a scoring point in the battle of wits

161   *flat-long*   with the flat side of the sword, not the point and therefore harmless

162   *mettle*   spirit, courage and a pun on metal swords

162–3   Gonzalo's sarcastic jibe is that Antonio and Sebastian could lift the moon out of its orbit, but only if it stayed still long enough to let them.

163   *sphere*   orbit.   *continue*   remain

S.D.   *Ariel*   He is invisible to the characters on stage.

164   *bat-fowling*   catching birds at night when they are roosting; fooling a simpleton

166   *adventure ... weakly*   risk losing my composure or judgement for so little reason. It seems Gonzalo has become weary of Antonio's and Sebastian's constant banter: but notice that they fail to get the better of him. What do you think is Gonzalo's opinion of these two?

167   *laugh me asleep*   put me to sleep with your laughing

168   *hear us*   hear us laugh

172   *omit the heavy offer*   disregard or neglect the opportunity of sleep

173   *It ... sorrow*   proverbial; 'Sleep rarely comes to one who grieves'

GONZALO	I would with such perfection govern, sir,	150

GONZALO I would with such perfection govern, sir,   150
          T'excel the Golden Age.

SEBASTIAN   'Save his Majesty!

ANTONIO Long live Gonzalo!

GONZALO   And – do you mark me, sir?

ALONSO Prithee, no more; thou dost talk nothing to me.

GONZALO I do well believe your Highness, and did it to minister occasion to
          these gentlemen, who are of such sensible and nimble lungs, that they   155
          always use to laugh at nothing.

ANTONIO 'Twas you we laughed at.

GONZALO Who in this kind of merry fooling am nothing to you: so you may
          continue, and laugh at nothing still.

ANTONIO What a blow was there given!   160

SEBASTIAN And it had not fallen flat-long.

GONZALO You are gentlemen of brave mettle; you would lift the moon out of
          her sphere if she would continue in it five weeks without changing.

Enter ARIEL, *invisible, playing solemn music*

SEBASTIAN We would so, and then go a bat-fowling.

ANTONIO Nay, good my lord, be not angry.   165

GONZALO No, I warrant you, I will not adventure my discretion so weakly.
          Will you laugh me asleep, for I am very heavy?

ANTONIO Go sleep, and hear us.

All sleep except ALONSO, SEBASTIAN *and* ANTONIO

ALONSO What, all so soon asleep? I wish mine eyes
          Would, with themselves, shut up my thoughts. I find   170
          They are inclined to do so.

SEBASTIAN   Please you, sir,
          Do not omit the heavy offer of it.
          It seldom visits sorrow; when it doth,
          It is a comforter.

ANTONIO   We two, my lord,
          Will guard your person while you take your rest,   175
          And watch your safety.

ALONSO   Thank you. Wondrous heavy...

ALONSO *falls asleep.*

[*Exit* ARIEL

SEBASTIAN What a strange drowsiness possesses them!

ANTONIO It is the quality o' the climate.

SEBASTIAN   Why

181   *as by* as if by

183   *No more* Antonio stops himself from continuing with his sinister suggestion

185   *th'occasion … thee* the opportunity is showing itself to you

187   *waking* awake

189   *sleepy language* a language which is incoherent or which is unbelievable

194–5   *wink'st … waking* you sleep whilst your eyes are open; you refuse to see

195   *distinctly* clearly

Does Sebastian understand Antonio's **sleepy language**?

How is the image of sleep built up and sustained?

How would you have the stage area arranged for this part of the scene (remember Ariel)?

197   *than my custom* than I usually am

199   *Trebles thee o'er* makes you three times greater than you are

199–201   The imagery changes to water. Sebastian says that he is 'standing' still whilst Antonio says he will teach him to move forward, to 'flow'. Sebastian admits that his natural inclination is to go backwards.

201   *Hereditary sloth* natural laziness or the laziness brought about by being the brother of the king

201–4   *O, … invest it* Antonio is telling Sebastian that although he banters ('mocks') around the subject ('purpose') of grasping the crown, he really does want ('cherish') it; and in rejecting or turning away from it ('stripping'), the more important it ('the purpose') becomes. The word 'invest' relates to the investiture of a king.

204   *Ebbing men* men who are going backwards or going nowhere

205   *near the bottom* the bottom of the ocean, hidden in the depths. *run* stay, live

206   *by* because of

207   *setting* expression

208   *matter* reason or purpose to be spoken of. *birth* the birth of an idea or pronouncement

209   *throes* to throe is to agonise in childbirth

210   *this lord* Gonzalo. *weak remembrance* poor memory due to old age

211   *little memory* little remembered

212   *earthed* buried

Doth it not then our eyelids sink? I find not
Myself disposed to sleep.

ANTONIO   Nor I; my spirits are nimble.   **180**
They fell together all, as by consent;
They dropped, as by a thunder-stroke. What might,
Worthy Sebastian …? O, what might …? No more.
And yet methinks I see it in thy face,
What thou shouldst be: th'occasion speaks thee, and   **185**
My strong imagination sees a crown
Dropping upon thy head.

SEBASTIAN   What? Art thou waking?

ANTONIO   Do you not hear me speak?

SEBASTIAN   I do, and surely
It is a sleepy language, and thou speak'st
Out of thy sleep. What is it thou didst say?   **190**
This is a strange repose, to be asleep
With eyes wide open; standing, speaking, moving,
And yet so fast asleep.

ANTONIO   Noble Sebastian,
Thou let'st thy fortune sleep – die rather; wink'st
Whiles thou art waking.

SEBASTIAN   Thou dost snore distinctly: **195**
There's meaning in thy snores.

ANTONIO   I am more serious than my custom: you
Must be so too, if heed me; which to do,
Trebles thee o'er.

SEBASTIAN   Well, I am standing water.

ANTONIO   I'll teach you how to flow.

SEBASTIAN   Do so. To ebb   **200**
Hereditary sloth instructs me.

ANTONIO   O,
If you but knew how you the purpose cherish
Whiles thus you mock it; how in stripping it
You more invest it. Ebbing men, indeed,
Most often do so near the bottom run   **205**
By their own fear or sloth.

SEBASTIAN   Prithee say on.
The setting of thine eye and cheek proclaim
A matter from thee; and a birth indeed
Which throes thee much to yield.

ANTONIO   Thus, sir:
Although this lord of weak remembrance, this   **210**
Who shall be of as little memory
When he is earthed, hath here almost persuaded –

213 *spirit of persuasion* essential power or ability to persuade

213–14 *only … persuade* Gonzalo's only profession, as a councillor, was to advise and persuade.

217–21 Antonio is saying that from the 'no hope' that Ferdinand is 'undrowned', there arises a 'great hope' and a 'high hope' which even Ambition could not see beyond, ie the hope of the crown and the deed necessary to achieve this can be done without discovery. This is another difficult speech, dense and complex in its syntax. Antonio is trying to persuade Sebastian to kill his brother, he is agitated, as we have seen Prospero agitated, and the syntax reflects this.

225 *Ten leagues* About 30 miles literally, but the phrase means 'a long way away'.

226 *no note* no communication, no letter. *post* postman, messenger

227 *too slow* the man in the moon takes a month to circle the earth, the sun takes 24 hours

227–8 *new-born … razorable* the time it takes a male child to grow into a man

228 *she that from whom* coming away from Claribel's wedding

229 *sea-swallowed* drowned. *cast* cast ashore, also a pun on being cast in a play, as are 'perform' and 'prologue'

230 *destiny* the fateful act of being saved

231 *past is prologue* the past is a preparation for what is to come, Sebastian being king

231–2 *what to … discharge* the future is up to us

232 *stuff* nonsense

235 *cubit* the length of a forearm, about 18 inches

237 *measure us* travel, return. *Keep* stay

238 *wake* wake himself up, stir himself. *death* Alonso and Gonzalo, being asleep, are as like being dead

240 *there be that* there are others that

241 *prate* chatter foolishly

243–4 *make … chat* teach to speak as much sense

244 *bore* shared

247 *content* contentment with what you have understood, and the content of it

248 *Tender* translate into, yield up

For he's a spirit of persuasion, only
Professes to persuade – the King his son's alive,
'Tis as impossible that he's undrowned   215
As he that sleeps here, swims.

SEBASTIAN   I have no hope
That he's undrowned.

ANTONIO   O, out of that no hope,
What great hope have you? No hope that way is
Another way so high a hope that even
Ambition cannot pierce a wink beyond,   220
But doubt discovery there. Will you grant with me
That Ferdinand is drowned?

SEBASTIAN   He's gone.

ANTONIO   Then tell me,
Who's the next heir of Naples?

SEBASTIAN   Claribel.

ANTONIO   She that is Queen of Tunis; she that dwells
Ten leagues beyond man's life; she that from Naples   225
Can have no note, unless the sun were post –
The man i' the moon's too slow – till new-born chins
Be rough and razorable; she that from whom
We all were sea-swallowed, though some cast again,
And that by destiny, to perform an act   230
Whereof what's past is prologue; what to come
In yours and my discharge.

SEBASTIAN   What stuff is this? How say you?
'Tis true my brother's daughter's Queen of Tunis;
So is she heir of Naples; 'twixt which regions
There is some space.

ANTONIO   A space whose every cubit   235
Seems to cry out, 'How shall that Claribel
Measure us back to Naples? Keep in Tunis,
And let Sebastian wake.' Say this were death
That now hath seized them, why, they were no worse
Than now they are. There be that can rule Naples   240
As well as he that sleeps; lords that can prate
As amply and unnecessarily
As this Gonzalo; I myself could make
A chough of as deep chat. O, that you bore
The mind that I do! What a sleep were this   245
For your advancement! Do you understand me?

SEBASTIAN   Methinks I do.

ANTONIO   And how does your content
Tender your own good fortune?

250   *garments*   royal robes

251   *feater*   more befitting

252   *fellows*   companions.   *men*   servants

254   *kibe*   a heel blister

255   *put me to*   force me to wear

256   *deity*   conscience

257   *candied*   sweetened as in sugared or, possibly, congealed

258   *molest*   annoy, get in the way

261   *steel*   sword

262–5   *whiles you … our course*   Antonio mimes the action which Sebastian must do, to close Gonzalo's eyes forever.

264   *morsel*   piece of flesh

265   *all the rest*   the rest of the courtiers

266   *take suggestion*   do as we say.   *cat laps milk*   proverbial; naturally and with enjoyment

267–8   *tell … hour*   agree to anything we propose

271   *tribute*   The annual amount paid by Antonio to Alonso; see Act 1 Scene 2, lines 112–15.

273   *rear*   raise

274   *fall it*   let it fall

276   *his friend*   ie Gonzalo

277   *project*   plan

284   *be sudden*   be quick

Why are you drawn?
Wherefore this ghastly looking?

60

SEBASTIAN   I remember
    You did supplant your brother Prospero.

ANTONIO   True;   **250**
    And look how well my garments sit upon me,
    Much feater than before; my brother's servants
    Were then my fellows, now they are my men.

SEBASTIAN   But for your conscience.

ANTONIO   Ay, sir: where lies that? If 'twere a kibe
    'Twould put me to my slipper; but I feel not   **255**
    This deity in my bosom; twenty consciences
    That stand 'twixt me and Milan, candied be they,
    And melt, ere they molest. Here lies your brother,
    No better than the earth he lies upon,
    If he were that which now he's like, that's dead;   **260**
    Whom I, with this obedient steel, three inches of it,
    Can lay to bed for ever; whiles you, doing thus,
    To the perpetual wink for aye might put
    This ancient morsel, this Sir Prudence, who
    Should not upbraid our course. For all the rest,   **265**
    They'll take suggestion as a cat laps milk;
    They'll tell the clock to any business that
    We say befits the hour.

SEBASTIAN   Thy case, dear friend,
    Shall be my precedent; as thou got'st Milan,
    I'll come by Naples. Draw thy sword, one stroke   **270**
    Shall free thee from the tribute which thou payest,
    And I, the King, shall love thee.

ANTONIO   Draw together;
    And when I rear my hand, do you the like,
    To fall it on Gonzalo.

SEBASTIAN   O, but one word.

He takes ANTONIO *aside to talk. Enter* ARIEL *with music and song*

ARIEL   My master through his Art foresees the danger   **275**
    That you, his friend, are in, and sends me forth –
    For else his project dies – to keep them living.

ARIEL *sings in* GONZALO'S *ear*

    While you here do snoring lie,
    Open-eyed Conspiracy
      His time doth take.   **280**
    If of life you keep a care,
    Shake off slumber and beware:
      Awake, awake!

ANTONIO   [*To* SEBASTIAN] Then let us both be sudden.

286 *you* your swords
287 *ghastly* full of fear
288 *securing* guarding
295 *humming* Ariel's singing
299 *verily* true

How do the words Sebastian uses in the speech beginning on line 288 show that he is lying?

How would you ask the actor playing Ariel to move at the end of the scene? Consider the idea that Ariel might have been on stage all along.

What important aspects of Ariel's character have been established at this point in the play?

Look back at the first scene of the play. What were your first impressions of Gonzalo, Sebastian and Antonio?

Write down the reasons why those first impressions have been confirmed or have changed.

By the end of this scene our understanding of the characters of the individuals stranded on the island is clearer. We see the grief of Alonso, the kindness and essential goodness of Gonzalo, the manipulative cruelty and treachery of Antonio and the gullibility of the not-so-bright Sebastian. The language has varied, from short, sharp repartee to the longer, poetic speeches of Francisco and Gonzalo.

2:2

Caliban hides beneath his cloak on seeing Trinculo, the jester, who joins him to shelter from the storm. The drunken Stephano discovers them both and Caliban delights in wine and thoughts of freedom.

1 *infections* germs, sick-making influences
2 *bogs ... flats* marsh or swamp
3 *inch-meal* inch by inch, as in piecemeal
4 *nor* neither
5 *urchin-shows* 'urchin' may mean elf or sprite; it was also an ancient name for a hedgehog
6 *firebrand* a light, a phosphorescence
9 *mow* grimace
11 *my barefoot way* the way along which I travel barefoot. *mount* raise

GONZALO   [*Waking, and rousing* ALONSO] Now good angels preserve the King!   **285**

                                                [*The others wake*

ALONSO   Why, how now, hoa; awake? Why are you drawn?
     Wherefore this ghastly looking?

GONZALO   What's the matter?

SEBASTIAN   Whiles we stood here securing your repose,
     Even now, we heard a hollow burst of bellowing,
     Like bulls, or rather lions; did't not wake you?   **290**
     It struck mine ear most terribly.

ALONSO   I heard nothing.

ANTONIO   O, 'twas a din to fright a monster's ear,
     To make an earthquake; sure it was the roar
     Of a whole herd of lions.

ALONSO   Heard you this, Gonzalo?

GONZALO   Upon mine honour, sir, I heard a humming,   **295**
     And that a strange one too, which did awake me.
     I shaked you, sir, and cried; as mine eyes opened,
     I saw their weapons drawn. There was a noise,
     That's verily. 'Tis best we stand upon our guard,
     Or that we quit this place; let's draw our weapons.   **300**

ALONSO   Lead off this ground, and let's make further search
     For my poor son.

GONZALO   Heavens keep him from these beasts,
     For he is sure i' th' island.

ALONSO   Lead away.

ARIEL   Prospero my lord shall know what I have done.
     So, King, go safely on to seek thy son.   **305**

                                        [*Exeunt*

2:2   *Enter* CALIBAN *with a burden of wood. A noise of thunder heard*

CALIBAN   All the infections that the sun sucks up
     From bogs, fens, flats, on Prosper fall, and make him
     By inch-meal a disease. His spirits hear me,
     And yet I needs must curse. But they'll nor pinch,
     Fright me with urchin-shows, pitch me i' the mire,   **5**
     Nor lead me like a firebrand in the dark
     Out of my way, unless he bid 'em; but
     For every trifle are they set upon me;
     Sometime like apes, that mow and chatter at me,
     And after bite me; then like hedgehogs, which   **10**
     Lie tumbling in my barefoot way, and mount
     Their pricks at my footfall; sometime am I

13   *wound* twined about with   *adders* vipers, poisonous snakes

16   *fall flat* hide flat on the ground

17   *Perchance* perhaps

18   *bear off* ward off

20   *bombard* Originally a cannon and then a leather vessel for carrying liquor, probably of similar shape.

25   *poor-John* dried fish

26   *had ... painted* Trinculo suggests that in England Caliban might be exhibited at a fair as a kind of freak; a painted board would advertise the attraction. *holiday fool* a person on holiday easily fooled into spending money

27   *monster make a man* a pun; the phrase can mean to attain the status of man and also make a man's fortune

28   *doit* small coin

29   *dead Indian* Indians, here meaning people from the West Indies, were brought back to England and, for a fee, displayed. *Legged* with legs

31   *let loose* let go of, revise

33   *gaberdine* cloak

34–5   *Misery ... bedfellows* proverbial; misery makes strange bedfellows

35   *shroud* take shelter. *dregs* last drops of the 'bombard' of line 20

38   *scurvy* low, contemptible

40   *the swabber* one who washes the decks and keeps the ship clean

44   *tang* sting

45   *Go hang* proverbial; 'Go to the devil'

47   *tailor ... itch* Kate would sleep with a tailor but not with a sailor

All wound with adders, who with cloven tongues
Do hiss me into madness.

Enter TRINCULO

Lo, now, lo!

Here comes a spirit of his, and to torment me   **15**
For bringing wood in slowly. I'll fall flat;
Perchance he will not mind me.

TRINCULO   Here's neither bush nor shrub to bear off any weather at all. And
another storm brewing; I hear it sing i' the wind. Yond same black
cloud, yond huge one, looks like a foul bombard that would shed his   **20**
liquor. If it should thunder as it did before, I know not where to hide my
head: yond same cloud cannot choose but fall by pailfuls. [*Notices
CALIBAN*] What have we here, a man or a fish? Dead or alive? A fish, he
smells like a fish; a very ancient and fish-like smell; a kind of … not of
the newest poor-John; a strange fish. Were I in England now, as once I   **25**
was, and had but this fish painted, not a holiday fool there but would
give a piece of silver. There would this monster make a man; any
strange beast there makes a man; when they will not give a doit to
relieve a lame beggar, they will lay out ten to see a dead Indian. Legged
like a man, and his fins like arms; [*Feels CALIBAN*] warm o' my troth! I do **30**
now let loose my opinion, hold it no longer: this is no fish, but an
islander that hath lately suffered by a thunderbolt. [*More thunder*] Alas,
the storm is come again. My best way is to creep under his gaberdine;
there is no other shelter hereabout. Misery acquaints a man with
strange bedfellows; I will here shroud till the dregs of the storm be past.   **35**

He hides under CALIBAN'S *cloak. Enter* STEPHANO *singing, with a bottle*

STEPHANO   I shall no more to sea, to sea,
Here shall I die ashore –
This is a very scurvy tune to sing at a man's funeral; well, here's my
comfort.

He drinks from his bottle, then sings

The master, the swabber, the boatswain and I,   **40**
The gunner and his mate,
Loved Mall, Meg, and Marian, and Margery,
But none of us cared for Kate;
For she had a tongue with a tang,
Would cry to a sailor, 'Go hang!'   **45**
She loved not the savour of tar nor of pitch,
Yet a tailor might scratch her where'er she did itch.
Then to sea, boys, and let her go hang.
This is a scurvy tune too; but here's my comfort.

[*Drinks*

CALIBAN   Do not torment me. O!   **50**

65

51   *put tricks* play tricks

52   *men of Ind* men from the Indies; Indians, men from the New World

53–4   *As proper … ground* Stephano adapts the proverb, 'As fine a fellow as ever went on legs'

> What do you notice about the way verse and prose are written in this scene?
>
> What might this tell us about Shakespeare's view of the relative importance of Caliban's character?
>
> What can you say about the metrical form of Caliban's speeches in the scene?

55   *at nostrils* through the nostrils

57   *monster* an imaginary animal, partly brute and partly human

58   *ague* fever or chill that causes shivers. *should he learn* where can he have learned? *language* ostensibly Neapolitan, actually English

59   *recover* restore

61   *neat's leather* cowhide; the reference is proverbial: 'As good a man as ever trod on shoe leather'

63   *after the wisest* sensibly

65–6   *I will not … soundly* No price is too high for him. Stephano's first inclination, like Trinculo's, is to make money out of the monster.

66   *that hath him* who will have him. *soundly* dearly

68   *trembling* the effect of being 'possessed'; Trinculo is trembling with fear

70   *cat* the proverb 'Ale (liquor) that would make a cat speak' *shake* shake off

71   *You … friend* you do not know that I am your friend

72   *chaps* chops, jaws

75   *delicate* pleasant, delightful

77   *detract* argue

> Play-read the scene from line 49 to 78. Try to bring out the comic elements in the extract.
>
> How might you use voice for Caliban and actions for Trinculo under the cloak to maximise the comedy?

78   *help* cure. *Amen* that's quite enough for that mouth; so be it

81   *long spoon* proverbial; 'He must have a long spoon that will eat with the devil'

84   *lesser* shorter

85   *very* true

86   *siege* the word derives from 'sege' meaning 'seat'; here backside, perhaps excrement. *mooncalf* monstrosity formed imperfectly through the influence of the moon. *vent* bring forth

93   *turn me about* Trinculo is dancing Stephano around the stage. *not constant* unsettled because of the drink he has taken

| STEPHANO | What's the matter? Have we devils here? Do you put tricks upon's with savages and men of Ind? ha? I have not 'scaped drowning, to be afeard now of your four legs; for it hath been said, 'As proper a man as ever went on four legs cannot make him give ground;' and it shall be said so again, while Stephano breathes at nostrils. | 55 |

CALIBAN   The spirit torments me. O!

STEPHANO   This is some monster of the isle with four legs, who hath got, as I take it, an ague. Where the devil should he learn our language? I will give him some relief, if it be but for that. If I can recover him, and keep him tame, and get to Naples with him, he's a present for any emperor   60
that ever trod on neat's-leather.

CALIBAN   Do not torment me, prithee; I'll bring my wood home faster.

STEPHANO   He's in his fit now, and does not talk after the wisest. He shall taste of my bottle: if he have never drunk wine afore, it will go near to remove his fit. If I can recover him, and keep him tame, I will not take too much   65
for him; he shall pay for him that hath him, and that soundly.

CALIBAN   Thou dost me yet but little hurt; thou wilt anon, I know it by thy trembling; now Prosper works upon thee.

STEPHANO   Come on your ways; open your mouth; here is that which will give language to you, cat. Open your mouth; this will shake your shaking, I   70
can tell you, and that soundly. You cannot tell who's your friend; open your chaps again.

TRINCULO   I should know that voice: it should be – but he is drowned; and these are devils. O defend me!

STEPHANO   Four legs and two voices; a most delicate monster! His forward voice,   75
now, is to speak well of his friend; his backward voice is to utter foul speeches and to detract. If all the wine in my bottle will recover him, I will help his ague. Come. Amen! I will pour some in thy other mouth.

TRINCULO   Stephano!

STEPHANO   Doth thy other mouth call me? Mercy, mercy! This is a devil, and no   80
monster: I will leave him, I have no long spoon.

TRINCULO   Stephano! If thou beest Stephano, touch me, and speak to me, for I am Trinculo. Be not afeard: thy good friend Trinculo.

STEPHANO   If thou beest Trinculo, come forth; I'll pull thee by the lesser legs; if any be Trinculo's legs, these are they. Thou art very Trinculo indeed!   85
How cam'st thou to be the siege of this moon-calf? Can he vent Trinculos?

TRINCULO   I took him to be killed with a thunderstroke. But art thou not drowned, Stephano? I hope now thou art not drowned. Is the storm over-blown? I hid me under the dead moon-calf's gaberdine, for fear of   90
the storm. And art thou living, Stephano? O Stephano, two Neapolitans 'scaped?

STEPHANO   Prithee do not turn me about, my stomach is not constant.

94	*sprites*	spirits
95	*celestial*	heavenly
97	*butt of sack*	cask of wine
103	*duck*	a proverb distorted; to swim like a fish
104	*kiss the book*	Trinculo raises the bottle to his lips, 'to kiss the cup'.
105	*made like a goose*	shaped like a goose or waddling like one
110	*Out … was*	Stephano claims what other unscrupulous voyagers had deceived natives with, ie being descended from the moon.
113	*thy dog and thy bush*	According to superstition, the man in the moon was banished there, with his dog, for gathering brushwood on a Sunday.
115	*furnish*	supply
116	*by this good light*	by God's light; a mild oath. *afeard* afraid
117	*credulous*	easily fooled
118	*well drawn*	a good draught of wine, Caliban drinks deeply. *in good sooth* truly
121–2	*god's / asleep*	when Stephano is asleep
125	*laugh … death*	proverbial; to die laughing. *puppy-headed* stupid-looking, perhaps, rather than looking like a dog
127	*kiss*	kiss the bottle, take another drink

Trinculo insults and dislikes Caliban. To whom might he be making his remarks?

What actions might the actor playing Trinculo employ to emphasise the comedy of this scene?

68

| CALIBAN | [*Aside*] These be fine things, and if they be not sprites. That's a brave god, and bears celestial liquor. I will kneel to him. | 95 |

STEPHANO   How didst thou 'scape? How cam'st thou hither? Swear by this bottle how thou cam'st hither. I escaped upon a butt of sack, which the sailors heaved o'erboard, by this bottle (which I made of the bark of a tree with mine own hands, since I was cast ashore).

CALIBAN   I'll swear upon that bottle to be thy true subject, for the liquor is not   100
earthly.

STEPHANO   Here; swear then how thou escapedst.

TRINCULO   Swum ashore, man, like a duck: I can swim like a duck, I'll be sworn.

STEPHANO   Here, kiss the book. Though thou canst swim like a duck, thou art
made like a goose.   105

TRINCULO   O Stephano, hast any more of this?

STEPHANO   The whole butt, man; my cellar is in a rock by the sea-side, where
my wine is hid. How now, moon-calf, how does thine ague?

CALIBAN   Hast thou not dropped from heaven?

STEPHANO   Out o' the moon, I do assure thee. I was the man i' the moon, when   110
time was.

CALIBAN   I have seen thee in her, and I do adore thee; my mistress showed me
thee, and thy dog, and thy bush.

STEPHANO   Come, swear to that: kiss the book.

He gives CALIBAN *the bottle to drink*

I will furnish it anon with new contents. Swear!   115

TRINCULO   By this good light, this is a very shallow monster; I afeard of him? A
very weak monster! the man i' the moon! A most poor credulous
monster! Well drawn, monster, in good sooth!

CALIBAN   I'll show thee every fertile inch o' th' island;
And I will kiss thy foot. I prithee, be my god.   120

TRINCULO   By this light, a most perfidious and drunken monster! When's god's
asleep, he'll rob his bottle.

CALIBAN   I'll kiss thy foot. I'll swear myself thy subject.

STEPHANO   Come on, then; down and swear.

TRINCULO   I shall laugh myself to death at this puppy-headed monster: a most   125
scurvy monster! I could find in my heart to beat him –

STEPHANO   Come, kiss.

TRINCULO   – but that the poor monster's in drink. An abominable monster!

CALIBAN   I'll show thee the best springs; I'll pluck thee berries;
I'll fish for thee; and get thee wood enough.   130
A plague upon the tyrant that I serve!
I'll bear him no more sticks, but follow thee,
Thou wondrous man.

135 *crabs* crab-apples or, more likely, shellfish from rock pools

136 *pig-nuts* the tubers of edible woodland plants, or peanuts

137 *jay's nests* birds of fine plumage and here eggs to eat

138 *marmoset* a little monkey, described as having 'good meat'

139 *filberts* hazel nuts

140 *scamels* probably sea-mel, a bird and a delicacy, or possibly a shellfish

142 *inherit* take possession of, rule over

143 *bear my bottle* Trinculo has become the royal cup-bearer. *by and by* soon

146 *dams* building dams to catch fish

147 *firing* firewood. *at requiring* on demand

148 *scrape trenchering* clean the boards on which food was served; trenchering is a noun, as in 'housing'

149 *Cacaliban* possibly indicates intoxication or a rhythm fitting the song

150 *new master ... new man* proverbial; Caliban has a new master, Prospero will need a new servant

151 *high-day* day of celebration as in 'high days and holidays'

152 *brave* meant sarcastically

Remind yourself of the characters of Antonio and Sebastian. What similarities or parallels are there between them and Trinculo and Stephano?

Caliban promises many things to Stephano; how does this compare with his previous relationship with Prospero?

In this comic scene we meet the two remaining characters in the play. Caliban sees the possibility of releasing himself from his servitude to Prospero and the seeds of more treachery are sown. The main thematic and dramatic elements are poised, now, for development. The audience anticipates the unfolding of the love story, the treachery, the retribution and lots more magic.

TRINCULO   A most ridiculous monster, to make a wonder of a poor drunkard.

CALIBAN   I prithee let me bring thee where crabs grow;   **135**
And I with my long nails will dig thee pig-nuts;
Show thee a jay's nest, and instruct thee how
To snare the nimble marmoset; I'll bring thee
To clustering filberts, and sometimes I'll get thee
Young scamels from the rock. Wilt thou go with me?   **140**

STEPHANO   I prithee now, lead the way without any more talking. Trinculo, the
King and all our company else being drowned, we will inherit here.
Here, bear my bottle, fellow Trinculo; we'll fill him by and by again.

CALIBAN *sings drunkenly*

Farewell, master; farewell, farewell!

TRINCULO   A howling monster; a drunken monster.   **145**

CALIBAN   No more dams I'll make for fish,
Nor fetch in firing at requiring,
Nor scrape trenchering, nor wash dish.
'Ban, 'ban, Cacaliban
Has a new master; get a new man!   **150**
Freedom, high-day! high-day, freedom! freedom, high-day, freedom!

STEPHANO   O brave monster! lead the way.

[*Exeunt*

3:1

Ferdinand, having incurred Prospero's anger and been punished by being made to stack logs, undertakes his labour with thoughts full of Miranda. She consoles him and offers to assist him in his work. The lovers declare their love for each other and Prospero looks on with satisfaction.

1	*sports* activities, pastimes. *painful* laborious, hard work
1–2	*labour ... off* the pleasure compensates for the pain
2	*baseness* manual labour
3	*nobly undergone* undertaken with dignity. *matters* tasks
4	*ends* results. *mean* humble
5	*heavy* sorrowful. *odious* unpleasant
6	*quickens* makes alive
8	*crabbed* irritable
9	*harshness* severity
11	*sore* severe; *injunction* command
13	*executor* performer, one doing a task. *I forget* Ferdinand has stopped working and now reminds himself that he must resume.
15	*busiest* the thoughts of Miranda are most busy in his mind when he labours
16	*lightning* the recent storm from which Trinculo sheltered under Caliban's gabardine
19	*'Twill weep* wood exudes sap when it burns
21	*safe* safely out of the way
22	*discharge* finish
23	*strive* attempt, endeavour
24	*bear* carry
26	*crack my sinews* snap my tendons
31	*worm* little thing; meant affectionately. *infected* with love for Ferdinand
32	*visitation* visit

What contrasts this scene with the last one?

How would you describe the mood and tone? Is Miranda being deceitful?

Prospero overhears them. How would you position Prospero on stage in an Elizabethan theatre?

3:1   *Enter* FERDINAND, *bearing a log*

FERDINAND There be some sports are painful, and their labour
       Delight in them sets off; some kinds of baseness
       Are nobly undergone; and most poor matters
       Point to rich ends. This my mean task
       Would be as heavy to me as odious, but   5
       The mistress which I serve quickens what's dead,
       And makes my labours pleasures. O, she is
       Ten times more gentle than her father's crabbed;
       And he's composed of harshness. I must remove
       Some thousands of these logs, and pile them up,   10
       Upon a sore injunction; my sweet mistress
       Weeps when she sees me work, and says such baseness
       Had never like executor. I forget;
       But these sweet thoughts do even refresh my labours,
       Most busiest, when I do it.

      Enter MIRANDA. *At the same time,* PROSPERO *enters on an upper level,*
                  unseen by those below

MIRANDA   Alas, now pray you   15
       Work not so hard; I would the lightning had
       Burnt up those logs that thou'rt enjoined to pile;
       Pray set it down, and rest you. When this burns,
       'Twill weep for having wearied you. My father
       Is hard at study; pray now, rest yourself;   20
       He's safe for these three hours.
FERDINAND   O most dear mistress,
       The sun will set before I shall discharge
       What I must strive to do.
MIRANDA   If you'll sit down,
       I'll bear your logs the while. Pray give me that;
       I'll carry it to the pile.
FERDINAND   No, precious creature,   25
       I had rather crack my sinews, break my back,
       Than you should such dishonour undergo,
       While I sit lazy by.
MIRANDA   It would become me
       As well as it does you; and I should do it
       With much more ease, for my good will is to it,   30
       And yours it is against.
PROSPERO   *[Aside]*   Poor worm, thou art infected;
       This visitation shows it.

32 *wearily* weary

34 *by* near by

37 *hest* behest, command. *Admired* Miranda's name means 'worthy of wonder'.

38 *top of admiration* the best that there is to admire

39 *dearest* most valued

40 *eyed* looked at. *best regard* in an admiring way

41–2 *Th' harmony … ear* the sweet things they have said have made me willingly attentive

44–6 *but some defect … foil* the lady's defect spoiled her other good qualities

45 *owed* owned

47 *perfect* flawless. *peerless* unable to be matched

48 *creature's best* the best features of all women

50 *glass* mirror

50–2 *nor have I … father* Miranda, here, omits Caliban in her list of men.

52 *features* bodily shapes. *abroad* elsewhere in the world

53 *skilless* ignorant

53–4 *my modesty … dower* Miranda refers to her virginity, the most precious gift she can bring her husband to be

57 *like of* admire

58 *Something* a little. *precepts* instructions

There is a formality and reserve about what the lovers are saying to each other. How do their words, tone and possible actions show this?

59 *condition* social position

61 *I would not so* I wish it were not the case

62 *wooden slavery* the toil of carrying wood

63 *flesh-fly … mouth* Ferdinand is saying that he is as little inclined to be a wood slave as he is to let a fly lay its eggs in his mouth.

69 *kind event* a happy ending

70 *hollowly* falsely. *invert* turn upside down

71 *boded* promised. *mischief* something bad

MIRANDA	You look wearily.	

FERDINAND No, noble mistress, 'tis fresh morning with me
When you are by at night. I do beseech you –
Chiefly that I might set it in my prayers –   **35**
What is your name?

MIRANDA   Miranda – O my father,
I have broke your hest to say so!

FERDINAND   Admired Miranda,
Indeed the top of admiration, worth
What's dearest to the world! Full many a lady
I have eyed with best regard, and many a time   **40**
Th' harmony of their tongues hath into bondage
Brought my too diligent ear. For several virtues
Have I liked several women; never any
With so full soul, but some defect in her
Did quarrel with the noblest grace she owed,   **45**
And put it to the foil. But you, O you,
So perfect and so peerless, are created
Of every creature's best.

MIRANDA   I do not know
One of my sex; no woman's face remember,
Save from my glass mine own; nor have I seen   **50**
More that I may call men than you, good friend,
And my dear father. How features are abroad
I am skilless of; but, by my modesty,
The jewel in my dower, I would not wish
Any companion in the world but you;   **55**
Nor can imagination form a shape
Besides yourself to like of. But I prattle
Something too wildly, and my father's precepts
I therein do forget.

FERDINAND   I am in my condition
A prince, Miranda; I do think, a king –   **60**
I would not so! – and would no more endure
This wooden slavery than to suffer
The flesh-fly blow my mouth. Hear my soul speak:
The very instant that I saw you, did
My heart fly to your service, there resides   **65**
To make me slave to it, and for your sake
Am I this patient log-man.

MIRANDA   Do you love me?

FERDINAND O heaven, O earth, bear witness to this sound,
And crown what I profess with kind event
If I speak true; if hollowly, invert   **70**
What best is boded me, to mischief. I

75

72 *what* whatever

76 *that ... 'em* the love that is developing between them. Prospero will also have in mind any offspring they may produce, heirs to Naples and Milan.

79 *die to want* die for lack of

81 *bigger bulk* the increasing love and desire; expressed by continuing the pregnancy metaphor. *Hence* away with

82 *prompt* guide

84 *maid* virgin and servant; with deliberate ambiguity, Miranda re-asserts her virginity and declaims her determination to serve him. *fellow* wife

86 *My mistress* the lady who commands my heart

89 *bondage e'er of freedom* as willingly as one in bondage would embrace freedom

91 *A thousand thousand* a million farewells

> *Look at lines 89 and 90. What dramatic action might Ferdinand and Miranda perform to pledge their love?*
>
> *If Prospero and the audience are to see this to full effect, how would you stage it?*

93 *with all* by all that is going on

93–4 *but my ... more* but I couldn't be happier

96 *business appertaining* matters concerning these events

Look back to Act 1 Scene 2 and your impressions of Miranda at that point in the play. What has happened to her since?

She has shown a number of different sides of her personality and may be more complex than she seems. One aspect may be her determination. How does she display this?

With Prospero's invisible consent, the two lovers have made progress in their declarations and their intentions.

This scene of youthfulness, love and the honest revealing of romantic feelings, comes as a relief from the grotesque, drunken comedy of the scene before and the one coming next.

Beyond all limit of what else i' the world,
Do love, prize, honour you.

MIRANDA   I am a fool
        To weep at what I am glad of.

PROSPERO   [*Aside*]   Fair encounter
        Of two most rare affections. Heavens rain grace   75
        On that which breeds between 'em.

FERDINAND   Wherefore weep you?

MIRANDA   At mine unworthiness, that dare not offer
        What I desire to give; and much less take
        What I shall die to want. But this is trifling,
        And all the more it seeks to hide itself   80
        The bigger bulk it shows. Hence bashful cunning,
        And prompt me plain and holy innocence.
        I am your wife, if you will marry me;
        If not, I'll die your maid. To be your fellow
        You may deny me, but I'll be your servant   85
        Whether you will or no.

FERDINAND   My mistress, dearest,
        And I thus humble ever.

MIRANDA   My husband, then?

FERDINAND   Ay, with a heart as willing
        As bondage e'er of freedom. Here's my hand.

MIRANDA   And mine, with my heart in't. And now farewell   90
        Till half an hour hence.

FERDINAND   A thousand thousand.

                [*Exeunt* FERDINAND *and* MIRANDA, *in different directions*

PROSPERO   So glad of this as they I cannot be,
        Who are surprised with all, but my rejoicing
        At nothing can be more. I'll to my book,
        For yet ere supper-time must I perform   95
        Much business appertaining.

                                        [*Exit*

3:2

Caliban tries to persuade Stephano to murder Prospero, using Miranda as the bait. Ariel, in the guise of Trinculo's voice, causes much trouble and comedy. All are drunk; Stephano and Trinculo fall out but are reunited. Ariel, invisible, hears all.

Tell not me! When the butt is out we will drink water, not a drop before.

1   *Tell not me!* Don't tell me; either to stop drinking or that the drink is running out

2   *bear up and board 'em* a nautical expression here meaning 'get on with the drinking'

3   *folly* freak; the word refers to Caliban

3–4   *five / upon this isle* Caliban has spoken of Prospero and Miranda

4   *brained … us* addled with drinking

6–7   *set in / thy head* fixed, staring

8   *brave* fine, worthy; sarcastically meant

10   *For my part* in my case

11–12   *five-and- / thirty leagues* over 100 miles; Stephano exaggerates and contradicts his earlier story

13   *standard* flag, flagpole or flagbearer

14   *list* like, and also 'lean over' drunkenly. *no standard* not able to stand

15   *run* run away from the enemy

16   *go* walk. *lie like dogs* proverbial; 'To lie like dogs in a field', also not tell the truth

20   *in case* valiant enough. *jostle* confront, push out of the way

21   *debauched* low-life

25   *natural* fool, idiot

What is Trinculo's attitude towards Caliban? Why might this be?

What might the actor playing Trinculo do on stage to show this?

27   *keep … head* be careful what you say

28   *the next tree* you'll be hanged from the next tree

31   *suit* suggestion, proposal

32   *Marry* a mild oath, from 'By the Virgin Mary'

33   *sorcerer* a magician of the black arts

3:2   *Enter* CALIBAN, STEPHANO, *and* TRINCULO

STEPHANO   Tell not me! When the butt is out we will drink water, not a drop
before. Therefore bear up, and board 'em. Servant-monster, drink to me.

TRINCULO   Servant-monster? The folly of this island! They say there's but five
upon this isle; we are three of them; if th'other two be brained like us,
the state totters.   5

STEPHANO   Drink, servant-monster, when I bid thee; thy eyes are almost set in
thy head.

TRINCULO   Where should they be set else? He were a brave monster indeed if
they were set in his tail.

STEPHANO   My man-monster hath drowned his tongue in sack. For my part the   10
sea cannot drown me; I swam, ere I could recover the shore, five-and-
thirty leagues off and on. By this light, thou shalt be my lieutenant,
monster, or my standard.

TRINCULO   Your lieutenant, if you list; he's no standard.

STEPHANO   We'll not run, Monsieur Monster.   15

TRINCULO   Nor go neither; but you'll lie like dogs, and yet say nothing neither.

STEPHANO   Moon-calf, speak once in thy life, if thou beest a good moon-calf.

CALIBAN   How does thy honour? Let me lick thy shoe; I'll not serve him, he is
not valiant.

TRINCULO   Thou liest, most ignorant monster; I am in case to jostle a constable.   20
Why, thou debauched fish, thou, was there ever man a coward that hath
drunk so much sack as I today? Wilt thou tell a monstrous lie, being but
half a fish and half a monster?

CALIBAN   Lo, how he mocks me; wilt thou let him, my lord?

TRINCULO   'Lord,' quoth he? That a monster should be such a natural!   25

CALIBAN   Lo, lo, again. Bite him to death, I prithee.

STEPHANO   Trinculo, keep a good tongue in your head. If you prove a mutineer,
the next tree! The poor monster's my subject, and he shall not suffer
indignity.

CALIBAN   I thank my noble lord. Wilt thou be pleased to hearken once again to   30
the suit I made to thee?

STEPHANO   Marry will I. Kneel and repeat it; I will stand, and so shall Trinculo.

Enter ARIEL, *invisible*

CALIBAN   As I told thee before, I am subject to a tyrant, a sorcerer, that by his
cunning hath cheated me of the island.

ARIEL   Thou liest.   35

CALIBAN   [*To* TRINCULO] 'Thou liest,' thou jesting monkey, thou?
I would my valiant master would destroy thee.
I do not lie.

40 *supplant* dislodge, remove, also usurp

41–2 *I … Mum* keep silent; from the proverb, 'I will say nothing but mum'

46 *this thing* Trinculo

49 *compassed* accomplished. *the party* the person, Prospero

51 *knock … head* biblical; Jael hammered a nail into Sisera's temples

53 *pied* many-coloured, as the garment worn by a jester. *ninny* simpleton. *patch* Patch was the name of Cardinal Wolsey's domestic fool

56 *brine* salt water

57 *quick freshes* quick-flowing fresh water

59 *turn … doors* banish any feelings of mercy

60 *stock-fish* dried cod or other fish were beaten before cooking

65 *give me the lie* accuse me of lying

66 *pox* a popular, unpleasant oath

67 *this can … do* this is the result of drinking sack. *murrain* a plague of pestilence

76 *seized his books* taken away his power

77 *paunch* stab in the stomach

78 *wezand* windpipe

STEPHANO Trinculo, if you trouble him any more in's tale, by this hand, I will
supplant some of your teeth.   **40**

TRINCULO Why, I said nothing.

STEPHANO Mum then, and no more. Proceed.

CALIBAN I say by sorcery he got this isle;
From me he got it. If thy Greatness will,
Revenge it on him, for I know thou dar'st,   **45**
But this thing dare not.

STEPHANO That's most certain.

CALIBAN Thou shalt be lord of it, and I'll serve thee.

STEPHANO How now shall this be compassed? Canst bring me to the party?

CALIBAN Yea, yea, my lord, I'll yield him thee asleep,   **50**
Where thou mayst knock a nail into his head.

ARIEL Thou liest, thou canst not.

CALIBAN What a pied ninny's this? Thou scurvy patch!
I do beseech thy Greatness, give him blows,
And take his bottle from him. When that's gone,   **55**
He shall drink naught but brine, for I'll not show him
Where the quick freshes are.

STEPHANO Trinculo, run into no further danger. Interrupt the monster one
word further, and by this hand, I'll turn my mercy out o' doors, and
make a stock-fish of thee.   **60**

TRINCULO Why, what did I? I did nothing. I'll go farther off.

STEPHANO Didst thou not say he lied?

ARIEL Thou liest.

STEPHANO Did I so? Take thou that! [*Beats* **TRINCULO**]
As you like this, give me the lie another time.   **65**

TRINCULO I did not give the lie. Out o' your wits, and hearing too? A pox o'
your bottle, this can sack and drinking do. A murrain on your monster,
and the devil take your fingers!

CALIBAN Ha, ha, ha!

STEPHANO [*To* **CALIBAN**] Now forward with your tale.   **70**
[*To* **TRINCULO**] Prithee stand further off.

CALIBAN Beat him enough. After a little time
I'll beat him too.

STEPHANO   Stand farther. [*To* **CALIBAN**]
                                      Come, proceed.

CALIBAN Why, as I told thee, 'tis a custom with him
I' th' afternoon to sleep. There thou mayst brain him,   **75**
Having first seized his books; or with a log
Batter his skull, or paunch him with a stake,
Or cut his wezand with thy knife. Remember

81

80 *sot* fool

> *Explain how you would stage Ariel's movements as he mimics Trinculo about the stage.*
>
> *Stephano is 'lording' the situation, asserting authority despite being drunk; how might he use the stage space to emphasis this?*

82 *rootedly* firmly, fundamentally. *but* only or especially

83 *brave útensils* impressive equipment, possibly used in alchemy or just household goods

84 *deck* decorate

87 *nonpareil* without equal

88 *dam* mother

90 *brave* splendid

91 *become* grace, adorn

92 *brood* children

94 *viceroys* deputies

95 *plot* scheme, conspiracy but also, perhaps, a reference to the play

103 *jocund* cheerful, merry. *troll the catch* sing the round in full

104 *while-ere* a short time ago

105 *do reason* do anything reasonable

107 *cout* make a fool of

108 *scout* mock, deride

109 *Thought is free* a proverbial saying

S.D. *tabor* a small drum played with one hand, the pipe in the other

112 *picture of Nobody* nobody who can be seen

114 *take't ... list* do as you will

	First to possess his books, for without them	
	He's but a sot, as I am, nor hath not	80

First to possess his books, for without them
He's but a sot, as I am, nor hath not   80
One spirit to command; they all do hate him
As rootedly as I. Burn but his books.
He has brave útensils (for so he calls them)
Which, when he has a house, he'll deck withal.
And that most deeply to consider is   85
The beauty of his daughter. He himself
Calls her a nonpareil; I never saw a woman
But only Sycorax, my dam, and she;
But she as far surpasseth Sycorax,
As great'st does least.

STEPHANO   Is it so brave a lass?   90

CALIBAN   Ay, lord, she will become thy bed, I warrant,
And bring thee forth brave brood.

STEPHANO   Monster, I will kill this man; his daughter and I will be King and
Queen – save our Graces! – and Trinculo and thyself shall be viceroys.
Dost thou like the plot, Trinculo?   95

TRINCULO   Excellent.

STEPHANO   Give me thy hand; I am sorry I beat thee; but while thou livest keep
a good tongue in thy head.

CALIBAN   Within this half hour will he be asleep;
Wilt thou destroy him then?

STEPHANO   Ay, on mine honour.   100

ARIEL   [*Aside*] This will I tell my master.

CALIBAN   Thou mak'st me merry; I am full of pleasure;
Let us be jocund. Will you troll the catch
You taught me but while-ere?

STEPHANO   At thy request, monster, I will do reason, any reason. Come on,   105
Trinculo, let us sing.

He sings

Flout 'em and cout 'em
And scout 'em and flout 'em;
Thought is free.

CALIBAN   That's not the tune.   110

ARIEL *plays the tune on a tabor and pipe*

STEPHANO   What is this same?

TRINCULO   This is the tune of our catch, played by the picture of Nobody.

STEPHANO   If thou beest a man, show thyself in thy likeness. If thou beest a
devil, take't as thou list.

TRINCULO   O, forgive me my sins!   115

83

116	*He ... debts* proverbial; 'Death pays all debts'
121	*airs* tunes
122	*twangling* an invented onomatopoeia
132	*by and by* soon
134	*see this taborer* the tabor-player, Ariel, who is invisible
136	*Wilt come?* Trinculo follows Stephano who is following the music. Caliban wants them to follow him to Prospero's cell.

Look again at Caliban's speech on lines 120–8, noticing how poetic it is. The diction and tone require a very different dramatic performance from the actor than many of Caliban's cursings.

Consider how this speech should be performed, then recite it accordingly.

Look back to Act 2 Scene 1 where Antonio tries to persuade Sebastian to kill Alonso. Compare his method of persuasion, reasons and language with Caliban's attempt to persuade Stephano to murder Prospero in this scene.

On line 92 Caliban tells Stephano that Miranda shall **bring thee forth brave brood**. Which of Caliban's own lines in Act 1 Scene 2 does this remind you of?

The themes of treachery, murder and usurpation are reinforced in this scene, which also provides the audience with humour, trickery and some gentle poetry from the complex and central character of Caliban.

3:3

Prospero provides a banquet for the weary courtiers but whisks it away just as they are about to eat. The vision is replaced by Ariel, in disguise, who reminds them of the wrongs of their past. Alonso feels guilt, Gonzalo is amazed, Antonio and Sebastian are aggressive.

1	*By'r lakin* by our Ladykin; a mild oath
2	*aches* ache. *Here's ... trod* we're lost, as in a maze
3	*forth-rights* paths that are straight. *meanders* paths that are crooked
5	*attached with* seized by
7	*Even here* here and now
8	*flatterer* deceiver
10	*frustrate* frustrated, thwarted
12	*repulse* setback, reversal. *purpose* the intention to kill Alonso

STEPHANO   He that dies pays all debts. I defy thee.
        Mercy upon us!

CALIBAN   Art thou afeard?

STEPHANO   No, monster, not I.

CALIBAN   Be not afeard; the isle is full of noises,   120
        Sounds and sweet airs, that give delight and hurt not.
        Sometimes a thousand twangling instruments
        Will hum about mine ears; and sometimes voices,
        That if I then had waked after long sleep,
        Will make me sleep again; and then, in dreaming,   125
        The clouds methought would open, and show riches
        Ready to drop upon me, that when I waked
        I cried to dream again.

STEPHANO   This will prove a brave kingdom to me, where I shall have my music
        for nothing.   130

CALIBAN   When Prospero is destroyed.

STEPHANO   That shall be by and by: I remember the story.

TRINCULO   The sound is going away; let's follow it, and after do our work.

STEPHANO   Lead, monster, we'll follow. I would I could see this taborer, he lays
        it on.   135

TRINCULO   Wilt come? I'll follow Stephano.

                                          [*Exeunt*

3:3   *Enter* ALONSO, SEBASTIAN, ANTONIO, GONZALO, ADRIAN,
            FRANCISCO, *and other* COURTIERS

GONZALO   By'r lakin, I can go no further, sir;
        My old bones aches. Here's a maze trod indeed
        Through forth-rights and meanders; by your patience,
        I needs must rest me.

ALONSO   Old lord, I cannot blame thee,
        Who am myself attached with weariness   5
        To the dulling of my spirits. Sit down and rest.
        Even here will I put off my hope, and keep it
        No longer for my flatterer: he is drowned
        Whom thus we stray to find, and the sea mocks
        Our frustrate search on land. Well, let him go.   10

ANTONIO   [*Aside to* SEBASTIAN] I am right glad that he's so out of hope.
        Do not for one repulse forego the purpose
        That you resolved t'effect.

14   *throughly* thoroughly

18   *harmony* music

20   *keepers* guardian angels. *were* the 'shapes' disappear quickly

21   *living drollery* a live puppet show with comic characters

22   *unicorns* mythological, horse-like beast with a single horn in its forehead

23–4 *There is … there* the phoenix is a mythological bird, reborn from the ashes of its own funeral pyre; only one exists at any time

25   *want credit* lack credibility

26   *Travellers* proverbial; 'A traveller may lie with authority' distorted by Antonio

30   *certes* certainly

*Notice that the stage direction puts Prospero **on the top**. How might this be done in the Elizabethan theatre? Where might you put him in a modern theatre?*

*There are also **strange shapes** bringing in the banquet. How would you have the individual characters react to the strange sights before them?*

31   *monstrous shape* Gonzalo refers to the 'strange shapes'

33   *human generation* the race of humans

36   *muse* wonder at

39   *Praise in departing* an ironic, proverbial observation from Prospero; guests should not compliment their host until they depart, since they do not fully know what is in store for them

41   *viands* food. *stomachs* appetites

SEBASTIAN   [*Aside to* ANTONIO] The next advantage
    Will we take throughly.

ANTONIO   [*Aside to* SEBASTIAN] Let it be tonight,
    For, now they are oppressed with travel, they   **15**
    Will not nor cannot use such vigilance
    As when they are fresh.

SEBASTIAN   [*Aside to* ANTONIO] I say tonight. No more.

Solemn and strange music; and PROSPERO *on the top, invisible. Enter several strange shapes, bringing in a banquet, and dance about it with gentle actions of salutations; and, inviting the King, etc., to eat, they depart*

ALONSO   What harmony is this? My good friends, hark!

GONZALO   Marvellous sweet music!

ALONSO   Give us kind keepers, heavens! What were these?   **20**

SEBASTIAN   A living drollery. Now I will believe
    That there are unicorns; that in Arabia
    There is one tree, the phoenix' throne, one phoenix
    At this hour reigning there.

ANTONIO   I'll believe both;
    And what does else want credit, come to me   **25**
    And I'll be sworn 'tis true. Travellers ne'er did lie,
    Though fools at home condemn 'em.

GONZALO   If in Naples
    I should report this now, would they believe me?
    If I should say I saw such islanders –
    For certes these are people of the island –   **30**
    Who though they are of monstrous shape, yet note
    Their manners are more gentle, kind, than of
    Our human generation you shall find
    Many, nay almost any.

PROSPERO   [*Aside*]   Honest lord,
    Thou hast said well: for some of you there present   **35**
    Are worse than devils.

ALONSO   I cannot too much muse
    Such shapes, such gesture, and such sound, expressing –
    Although they want the use of tongue – a kind
    Of excellent dumb discourse.

PROSPERO   [*Aside*]   Praise in departing.

FRANCISCO   They vanished strangely.

SEBASTIAN   No matter, since   **40**
    They have left their viands behind, for we have stomachs.
    Will't please you taste of what is here?

ALONSO   Not I.

44   *mountaineers*   people who live on mountains

45   *Dew-lapped*   with folds of skin

46   *wallets*   nodules of flesh

46–7   *men … breasts*   travellers' tales reported men whose heads grew beneath their shoulders

48   *putter-out*   one who puts on a bet; insurance brokers would bet against a traveller reaching his destination at odds of five to one

49   *warrant*   proof.   *stand to*   come forward

50   *Although … matter*   although it may be my last meal, it does not matter

S.D.   *harpy*   a mythical bird with a woman's head, talons for hands and the body of a vulture.   *quaint device*   inventive mechanical method of making the table disappear

53–6   *Destiny … on this island*   Destiny, who has control over the lower world and what is in it, has caused the sea to throw you up on to this island

53   *Destiny*   pre-ordained outcome

54   *to instrument*   control over

55   *never-surfeited*   never full up

59   *such-like valour*   the courage which comes from madness

60   *their proper selves*   their own persons

*How might you represent Ariel as a **harpy** for a modern or futuristic production of the play?*

What costume and props, eg weapons, might the other characters have in such a production?

How could you use computer technology for the special effects in this scene?

How might the strange shapes be an opportunity for dramatic spectacle?

61   *ministers*   agents, servants

61–4   *elements … waters*   metal from the earth, forged by fire into swords, has no power against wind (air) and water

62   *whom*   which

63   *bemocked-at*   scorned

64   *still-closing*   the waters of the sea will always close over (heal) any wounding stab made to it

65   *dowle*   one of the fibres of a feather

66   *like*   similarly.   *if*   even if

67   *massy*   heavy

69   *business*   mission; Ariel's task is to remind them of their past actions

71   *requit*   repaid, avenged

73   *Powers*   gods, but also Prospero's powers

74   *Incensed*   angered

76   *bereft*   taken away, also bereaved

77–8   *Lingering perdition … once*   long-lasting damnation, worse than a quick death

78   *attend*   follow

79   *wraths*   angers

81   *heart's sorrow*   repentance

82   *clear*   pure, blameless

GONZALO   Faith sir, you need not fear. When we were boys
             Who would believe that there were mountaineers
             Dew-lapped like bulls, whose throats had hanging at 'em   **45**
             Wallets of flesh? Or that there were such men
             Whose heads stood in their breasts? which now we find
             Each putter-out of five for one will bring us
             Good warrant of.

ALONSO   I will stand to, and feed;
             Although my last, no matter, since I feel   **50**
             The best is past. Brother, my lord the Duke,
             Stand to, and do as we.

             Thunder and lightning. Enter ARIEL *like a harpy, claps his wings upon the*
                   table, and with a quaint device the banquet vanishes

ARIEL   You are three men of sin, whom Destiny,
             That hath to instrument this lower world
             And what is in't, the never-surfeited sea   **55**
             Hath caused to belch up you; and on this island,
             Where man doth not inhabit, you 'mongst men
             Being most unfit to live, I have made you mad;
             And even with such-like valour men hang and drown
             Their proper selves.

                           They draw their swords

                           You fools, I and my fellows   **60**
             Are ministers of Fate; the elements
             Of whom your swords are tempered may as well
             Wound the loud winds, or with bemocked-at stabs
             Kill the still-closing waters, as diminish
             One dowle that's in my plume. My fellow-ministers   **65**
             Are like invulnerable; if you could hurt,
             Your swords are now too massy for your strengths,
             And will not be uplifted. But remember –
             For that's my business to you – that you three
             From Milan did supplant good Prospero,   **70**
             Exposed unto the sea, which hath requit it,
             Him, and his innocent child; for which foul deed,
             The Powers, delaying, not forgetting, have
             Incensed the seas and shores, yea, all the creatures
             Against your peace. Thee of thy son, Alonso,   **75**
             They have bereft, and do pronounce by me
             Lingering perdition, worse than any death
             Can be at once, shall step by step attend
             You and your ways; whose wraths to guard you from –
             Which here, in this most desolate isle, else falls   **80**
             Upon your heads – is nothing but heart's sorrow,
             And a clear life ensuing.

S.D.	*mocks and mows* grimacing, mocking facial expressions
83	*Bravely* splendidly, well done. *figure* shape, impersonation
84	*devouring* Ariel enacted the part with consummate grace.
85	*bated* omitted
86	*good life* liveliness, realistically
87	*observation strange* close attention to instructions. *meaner ministers* lesser servants who assist Ariel
88	*several kinds* various tasks. *high charms* magic of an elevated and complex kind
89	*knit up* confused, entangled
90	*distractions* madness
93	*mine* my
95	*strange stare* Alonso is mesmerised by what he has seen and heard, Gonzalo, being innocent, has not shared the same, strange experience.
96	*billows* waves of sound, or water. *it* the wrongdoing of Alonso's past
98	*deep* low-pitched
99	*bass my trespass* spoke in a low voice of my base sins; bass is also a pun on 'base'
100	*ooze* mud of the sea bed
101	*plummet* the plumb line used to measure the depth of water and fathom the sea bed
102–3	*But … legions o'er* if the devils come one at a time I'll fight them all
103	*second* helper
105	*poison … after* poison with a delayed effect
106	*bite the spirits* sap their strength and vitality, worry and confuse them
107	*of suppler joints* physically fitter
108	*hinder* stop, prevent. *ecstasy* madness, distraction

How could you show by movement and action that Ariel is in control?

How should the lines be read so that Alonso becomes 'distracted'?

How do you think Antonio and Sebastian should react as Ariel as speaking? They need to maintain their aggressive characteristics.

Look back at the appearances Ariel has made on stage. How many different moods and characteristics have you seen him portray?

Do you think that the characters in this scene have been consistent in attitude, mood and response to their situation throughout the play? Explain with some detail.

At this point in the play, which in terms of its five-act structure is just over half way, Prospero is beginning to move events towards their climax. The audience knows where all of the characters are situated on the island, and the state they are in. The play's duration is intended to coincide with the events of the action. Prospero said in Act 1 Scene 2, **The time twixt six and now / Must by us be spent most preciously.**

Prospero has accomplished much, but there is still much to do.

He vanishes in thunder; then, to soft music, enter the shapes again, and
dance, with mocks and mows, and carrying out the table

PROSPERO   Bravely the figure of this harpy hast thou
            Performed, my Ariel; a grace it had devouring.
            Of my instruction hast thou nothing bated   **85**
            In what thou hadst to say; so, with good life
            And observation strange, my meaner ministers
            Their several kinds have done. My high charms work,
            And these mine enemies are all knit up
            In their distractions: they now are in my power;   **90**
            And in these fits I leave them, while I visit
            Young Ferdinand, whom they suppose is drowned,
            And his and mine loved darling.   [*Exit*

GONZALO   I'the name of something holy, sir, why stand you
           In this strange stare?

ALONSO   O, it is monstrous, monstrous!   **95**
            Methought the billows spoke, and told me of it;
            The winds did sing it to me; and the thunder,
            That deep and dreadful organ-pipe, pronounced
            The name of Prosper: it did bass my trespass.
            Therefore my son i'th' ooze is bedded; and   **100**
            I'll seek him deeper than e'er plummet sounded,
            And with him there lie mudded.   [*Exit*

SEBASTIAN   But one fiend at a time,
            I'll fight their legions o'er.

ANTONIO   I'll be thy second.

                                    [*Exeunt* ANTONIO *and* SEBASTIAN

GONZALO   All three of them are desperate. Their great guilt,
            Like poison given to work a great time after,   **105**
            Now 'gins to bite the spirits. I do beseech you
            That are of suppler joints, follow them swiftly
            And hinder them from what this ecstasy
            May now provoke them to.

ADRIAN   Follow, I pray you.

                                    [*Exeunt*

91

4:1

Ferdinand passes the trials of his love set by Prospero and is rewarded with Miranda but with a stern warning concerning moral behaviour. A masque is presented for the couple but ends abruptly as Prospero remembers the plot against his life. Caliban tries to organise his hopeless companions, who are distracted by magic clothing.

1 *austerely* harshly

2 *compensation* reward

3 *third* Miranda is one third of Prospero's life; his art and his dukedom make up the rest

5 *vexations* labours

7 *strangely* admirably

8 *ratify* agree

9 *her off* as in 'show her off' or boast of her

11 *halt* limp

12 *Against an oracle* even if an oracle said otherwise

14 *purchased* won by toil

15 *virgin-knot* maidenhead

16 *sanctimonious* holy

17 *holy rite* marriage ceremony

18 *sweet aspersion* sprinkling or shower of blessings

19 *grow* blossom, but with reference to the coming of children

19–20 *Hate … Discord* The personifications are like characters in a masque, such as the one to come.

20–1 *bestrew … weeds* cover the marriage bed with weeds rather than the customary flowers

23 *Hymen's lamps* Hymen, god of marriage carried a torch which shone brightly on a happy union.

24 *fair issue* fine children

25 *murkiest den* darkest cave

26–7 *strongest … can* greatest temptation an evil spirit might make

29 *edge* enjoyment

30–1 *Phoebus … below* Ferdinand will not let lust take away the anticipation and enjoyment of the forthcoming marriage – when the sun will never seem to set because Phoebus's horses foundered, nor the wedding night ever seem to arrive because Night has been imprisoned.

30 *Phoebus* another name for Apollo, one of the most powerful of the Greek gods

33 *What, Ariel!* come, Ariel

34 *potent* powerful

35 *meaner fellows* lesser spirits who work for Ariel

37 *rabble* Ariel's helpers

4:1   *Enter* PROSPERO, FERDINAND, *and* MIRANDA

PROSPERO   If I have too austerely punished you,
              Your compensation makes amends, for I
              Have given you here a third of mine own life,
              Or that for which I live; who once again
              I tender to thy hand. All thy vexations   5
              Were but my trials of thy love, and thou
              Hast strangely stood the test. Here, afore heaven,
              I ratify this my rich gift. O Ferdinand,
              Do not smile at me that I boast her off,
              For thou shalt find she will outstrip all praise   10
              And make it halt behind her.

FERDINAND   I do believe it
              Against an oracle.

PROSPERO   Then, as my gift and thine own acquisition,
              Worthily purchased, take my daughter. But
              If thou dost break her virgin-knot before   15
              All sanctimonious ceremonies may
              With full and holy rite be ministered,
              No sweet aspersion shall the heavens let fall
              To make this contract grow; but barren Hate,
              Sour-eyed Disdain and Discord shall bestrew   20
              The union of your bed with weeds so loathly
              That you shall hate it both: therefore take heed,
              As Hymen's lamps shall light you.

FERDINAND   As I hope
              For quiet days, fair issue, and long life,
              With such love as 'tis now, the murkiest den,   25
              The most opportune place, the strong'st suggestion
              Our worser genius can, shall never melt
              Mine honour into lust, to take away
              The edge of that day's celebration
              When I shall think, or Phoebus' steeds are foundered,   30
              Or Night kept chained below.

PROSPERO   Fairly spoke.
              Sit then, and talk with her; she is thine own.
              What, Ariel! my industrious servant, Ariel!

                        Enter ARIEL

ARIEL   What would my potent master? Here I am.

PROSPERO   Thou and thy meaner fellows your last service   35
              Did worthily perform, and I must use you
              In such another trick. Go bring the rabble,
              O'er whom I give thee power, here, to this place.

39 *quick motion* be speedy

41 *vanity … Art* lighthearted display of magic

42 *Presently* immediately

43 *with a twink* in the winking of an eye

46 *tripping* moving nimbly

47 *mop and mow* grimace and pouting

49 *delicate* fine, exquisite

50 *conceive* understand

51 *dalliance* love play and conversation

52 *rein* freedom, indulgence

52–3 *strongest … blood* passion and desire can destroy good intention

53 *abstemious* moderate and controlled

54 *good night* farewell to

55–6 *white … liver* the cool purity of Ferdinand's heart mitigates his passion and desire

57 *corollary* additional helper

58 *want* lack. *pertly* quickly, smartly

59 *No tongue* stop talking

Ariel has helpers, meaner spirits, corollaries to assist him in his magical work for Prospero. How might you involve these spirits on stage during Ariel's speech and exit?

They should show speed, nimbleness and be **tripping** on their toes.

S.D. *Iris* goddess of the rainbow and Juno's messenger

60 *Ceres* goddess of the earth and of agriculture. *leas* fields, meadows

61 *vetches* coarse crops, tares, used to feed animals

62 *turfy* grassy

63 *meads thatched* meadows covered. *stover* grass

64 *pionèd and twillèd brims* the tops of the banks are trenched and woven with sticks to stop erosion

65 *spongy* wet, rainy. *hest* behest, command. *betrims* decks with spring flowers

66 *cold nymphs* nymphs who are not sexually aroused. *chaste crowns* coronets of flowers which symbolise virginity. *broomgroves* broom is a yellow-flowered shrub

67 *dismissed* rejected

68 *lass-lorn* without a girl. *poll-clipt* pruned

69 *sea-marge* seacoast

70 *Queen o' the sky* Juno

71 *watery arch* rainbow

72 *these* the fertile country described above

74 *peacocks* Juno's sacred birds, which draw her chariot. *amain* with speed

75 *entertain* welcome

Incite them to quick motion, for I must
Bestow upon the eyes of this young couple   **40**
Some vanity of mine Art: it is my promise,
And they expect it from me.

ARIEL   Presently?

PROSPERO   Ay; with a twink.

ARIEL   Before you can say 'come' and 'go,'
And breathe twice and cry 'so, so,'   **45**
Each one, tripping on his toe,
Will be here with mop and mow.
Do you love me, master? No?

PROSPERO   Dearly, my delicate Ariel. Do not approach
Till thou dost hear me call.

ARIEL   Well; I conceive.   [*Exit*   **50**

PROSPERO   Look thou be true; do not give dalliance
Too much the rein; the strongest oaths are straw
To the fire i' the blood; be more abstemious,
Or else, good night your vow!

FERDINAND   I warrant you, sir,
The white cold virgin snow upon my heart   **55**
Abates the ardour of my liver.

PROSPERO   Well.
Now come, my Ariel, bring a corollary,
Rather than want a spirit; appear, and pertly.

                            Soft music

No tongue; all eyes; be silent.

                            Enter **IRIS**

IRIS   *Ceres, most bounteous lady, thy rich leas*   **60**
Of wheat, rye, barley, vetches, oats and pease;
Thy turfy mountains, where live nibbling sheep,
And flat meads thatched with stover, them to keep;
Thy banks with pionèd and twillèd brims,
Which spongy April at thy hest betrims,   **65**
To make cold nymphs chaste crowns; and thy broom-groves,
Whose shadow the dismissèd bachelor loves,
Being lass-lorn; thy poll-clipt vineyard,
And thy sea-marge, sterile and rocky-hard,
Where thou thyself dost air – the Queen o' the sky,   **70**
Whose watery arch and messenger am I,
Bids thee leave these, and with her Sovereign Grace,
Here on this grass-plot, in this very place,
To come and sport. Her peacocks fly amain:
Approach, rich Ceres, her to entertain.   **75**

76   *many-coloured messenger* Iris, the messenger dressed in her rainbow robes

77   *wife of Jupiter* Juno; Jupiter was king of the gods

78   *saffron* yellow-coloured

79   *Diffusest honey-drops* shed sweet drops of rain

80   *blue bow* rainbow

81   *bosky acres* shrub-covered fields. *unshrubbed down* barren hills

82   *Rich scarf* colourful rainbow

83   *short-grassed green* the lawn prepared for dancing

85   *donation … estate* gift to generously bestow

86   *heavenly bow* Iris

87   *Venus … son* Venus, the goddess of love and Cupid, both associated with sexual desire, against which Prospero has warned Ferdinand

88–91   *Since they … forsworn* Ceres' daughter, Proserpina, was abducted by Dis, the god of the underworld, with the help of Venus and Cupid; there she stayed for six months of the year. Ceres now has nothing to do with their disgraceful company.

90   *blind boy* Cupid was often portrayed blindfolded; hence 'Love is blind'

As Ferdinand says on line 118, the masque has to be **a most majestic vision**. As producer in an Elizabethan or a modern theatre, how would you set the scene – what would you have on stage?

How would Iris and Ceres be brought on to the stage?

How might costume, lighting and music enhance this **majestic** scene?

92   *her Deity* herself, Venus

93   *Cutting … Paphos* speeding across the sky towards her home in Cyprus

94   *Dove-drawn* her chariot drawn by doves

94–5   *they … maid* they intended to strike Miranda and Ferdinand with Cupid's arrows and thus awaken sexual desire in them

96   *bed-right* consummation of marriage

97   *Till Hymen's … lighted* until they are married

98   *Mars's hot minion* Venus was Mars' lover

This is a most majestic vision.

99–100   *Her … no more* Cupid has broken his arrows and will no longer provoke desire

99   *waspish* ready to sting like a wasp

100   *sparrows* proverbial; 'As lustful as sparrows', so ironic in meaning

101   *boy right out* an outright boy, behave like a human child, not a god. *Highest Queen* Juno was queen of the gods and goddess of marriage

102   *gait* manner, deportment

104   *twain* couple

105   *issue* offspring

110   *foison* abundance

111   *garners* granaries

Enter CERES

CERES *Hail, many-coloured messenger, that ne'er*
Dost disobey the wife of Jupiter;
Who, with thy saffron wings, upon my flowers
Diffusest honey-drops, refreshing showers,
And with each end of thy blue bow dost crown   80
My bosky acres and my unshrubbed down,
Rich scarf to my proud earth; why hath thy Queen
Summoned me hither, to this short-grassed green?

IRIS *A contract of true love to celebrate,*
And some donation freely to estate   85
On the blest lovers.

CERES *Tell me, heavenly bow,*
If Venus or her son, as thou dost know,
Do now attend the Queen? Since they did plot
The means that dusky Dis my daughter got,
Her and her blind boy's scandalled company   90
I have forsworn.

IRIS *Of her society*
Be not afraid: I met her Deity
Cutting the clouds towards Paphos, and her son
Dove-drawn with her. Here thought they to have done
Some wanton charm upon this man and maid,   95
Whose vows are that no bed-right shall be paid
Till Hymen's torch be lighted; but in vain;
Mars's hot minion is returned again;
Her waspish-headed son has broke his arrows,
Swears he will shoot no more, but play with sparrows,   100
And be a boy right out.

CERES *Highest Queen of state,*
Great Juno comes; I know her by her gait.

Enter JUNO

JUNO *How does my bounteous sister? Go with me*
To bless this twain, that they may prosperous be
And honoured in their issue.   105

JUNO and CERES sing

JUNO *Honour, riches, marriage-blessing,*
Long continuance and increasing,
Hourly joys be still upon you!
Juno sings her blessings on you.

CERES *Earth's increase, foison plenty,*   110
Barns and garners never empty;
Vines with clustering bunches growing,

97

113   *burden bowing*   bowed down with the weight of fruit

114–15   *Spring … harvest*   may spring follow the harvest, thus removing the scarcities of winter

116   *shun*   ignore

119   *Harmonious charmingly*   as in charm or spell, charmed song

121   *their confines*   their natural places of rest, their element

123   *wondered father*   a father who performs wonders, a play on Miranda's name

The masque can be seen as a play within a play; celebrating the abundance of marriage but warning against lust.

How are Venus and Cupid presented here by Ceres and Iris?

To whom would they be addressing their words in performance?

125   *whisper*   the goddesses whisper instructions to Iris to prepare the next part of the masque

127   *marred*   spoiled

128   *nymphs*   semi-divine maidens.   *Naiads*   water nymphs. *windring*   winding, wandering, curving

129   *sedged crowns*   coronets woven from sedge, a water plant. *ever-harmless*   innocent

130   *crisp channels*   rippling waterways

132   *temperate*   chaste, virginal

134   *sicklemen*   harvesters who use sickles. *August weary*   the harvest is gathered in August

135   *furrow*   track made by a plough

136   *rye-straw*   rye is a cereal crop; 'cereal' comes from 'Ceres'

137   *encounter*   stand opposite

138   *footing*   dancing

S.D.   *habited*   dressed.   *heavily*   reluctantly or quickly

142   *avoid*   depart

143   *passion*   excitement, agitation

144   *works*   affects

145   *distempered*   troubled, out of humour

Plants with goodly burden bowing;
Spring come to you at the farthest
In the very end of harvest. 115
Scarcity and want shall shun you,
Ceres' blessing so is on you.

FERDINAND This is a most majestic vision, and
Harmonious charmingly. May I be bold
To think these spirits?

PROSPERO   Spirits, which by mine Art 120
I have from their confines called to enact
My present fancies.

FERDINAND   Let me live here ever;
So rare a wondered father and a wise
Makes this place Paradise.

JUNO and CERES whisper, and send IRIS on employment

PROSPERO   Sweet now, silence!
Juno and Ceres whisper seriously; 125
There's something else to do; hush, and be mute,
Or else our spell is marred.

IRIS   *You nymphs, called Naiads, of the windring brooks,*
With your sedged crowns, and ever-harmless looks,
Leave your crisp channels, and on this green land 130
Answer your summons; Juno does command.
Come, temperate nymphs, and help to celebrate
A contract of true love; be not too late.

Enter certain NYMPHS

You sun-burned sicklemen, of August weary,
Come hither from the furrow, and be merry, 135
Make holiday; your rye-straw hats put on,
And these fresh nymphs encounter every one
In country footing.

Enter certain REAPERS, properly habited; they join with the NYMPHS in a
graceful dance, towards the end whereof PROSPERO starts suddenly and
speaks, after which, to a strange, hollow and confused noise, they
heavily vanish

PROSPERO   [*Aside*] I had forgot that foul conspiracy
Of the beast Caliban and his confederates 140
Against my life: the minute of their plot
Is almost come. [*To the SPIRITS*] Well done! avoid; no more.

FERDINAND This is strange: your father's in some passion
That works him strongly.

MIRANDA   Never till this day
Saw I him touched with anger so distempered. 145

146   *in a moved sort* upset, concerned

148   *revels* entertainment; particularly the final dance between
       masquers and spectators

149   *foretold you* told you before

There's something else to do *says Prospero on line 126. What follows?
Who is dancing with whom?*

How would you have the actors respond to the sudden ending?

---

151   *baseless fabric* having no basis in reality, ethereal

152   *cloud-capped towers* towers so tall that they penetrate the clouds

153   *great globe* the world, but also the Globe playhouse where many
       of Shakespeare's plays were performed

154   *all ... inherit* everybody who will live in the world, and all who
       perform in or go to the Globe

155   *insubstantial pageant* unreal entertainment

156   *rack* trace, driven cloud which leaves no trace; also a frame
       We human kind, but also actors and entertainers

157   *on* of

158   *rounded ... sleep* completed by death

162   *turn* short stroll

163   *still* calm. *beating* turbulent

164   *with a thought* as swiftly as a thought

165   *cleave to* adhere to, obey to the letter

167   *presented* played the part of or organised the performance of

170   *varlets* scoundrels

171   *red-hot* red-faced, excitable, fired with false valour

172–3 *smote ... faces* The metaphor indicates how quarrelsome they
        were.

173   *beat the ground* walked heavily, staggered

174   *kissing* touching. *bending* aiming

176   *unbacked colts* wild, unbroken young horses

177   *advanced* raised

178   *As they smelt* as if they could smell

179   *calf-like* as docile as a calf. *lowing* the sound made by cattle

180   *Toothed* thorny. *sharp furzes* prickly shrubs. *pricking goss*
       sharp gorse

182   *filthy-mantled* covered with slime

184   *O'erstunk* stank worse than

Look at Ariel's speech on lines 167–9. What does the word **commander** *tell us?
Why might Ariel have been afraid? How many strands of the plot are moving
toward a climax? How has Ariel linked them?*

PROSPERO   You do look, my son, in a moved sort,
            As if you were dismayed: be cheerful, sir.
            Our revels now are ended; these our actors,
            As I foretold you, were all spirits, and
            Are melted into air, into thin air.   150
            And, like the baseless fabric of this vision,
            The cloud-capped towers, the gorgeous palaces,
            The solemn temples, the great globe itself,
            Yea, all which it inherit, shall dissolve,
            And, like this insubstantial pageant faded,   155
            Leave not a rack behind. We are such stuff
            As dreams are made on; and our little life
            Is rounded with a sleep. Sir, I am vexed;
            Bear with my weakness, my old brain is troubled;
            Be not disturbed with my infirmity.   160
            If you be pleased, retire into my cell,
            And there repose; a turn or two I'll walk,
            To still my beating mind.

FERDINAND *and* MIRANDA   We wish your peace.

                                                        [*Exeunt*

PROSPERO [*To* ARIEL, *who is off-stage*] Come with a thought! I thank thee, Ariel; come.

                        Enter ARIEL

ARIEL   Thy thoughts I cleave to. What's thy pleasure?

PROSPERO   Spirit,   165
            We must prepare to meet with Caliban.

ARIEL   Ay, my commander, when I presented Ceres
            I thought to have told thee of it, but I feared
            Lest I might anger thee.

PROSPERO   Say again, where didst thou leave these varlets?   170

ARIEL   I told you, sir, they were red-hot with drinking,
            So full of valour that they smote the air
            For breathing in their faces; beat the ground
            For kissing of their feet; yet always bending
            Towards their project. Then I beat my tabor,   175
            At which like unbacked colts they pricked their ears,
            Advanced their eyelids, lifted up their noses
            As they smelt music; so I charmed their ears
            That, calf-like, they my lowing followed through
            Toothed briers, sharp furzes, pricking goss and thorns, 180
            Which entered their frail shins; at last I left them
            I' the filthy-mantled pool beyond your cell,
            There dancing up to the chins, that the foul lake
            O'erstunk their feet.

184 *my bird* an affectionate term and reminder of Ariel's ability to fly

186 *trumpery* fancy but worthless garments

187 *stale* bait; could also mean trash

188 *nature* the effect of genetic make-up on a person's behaviour

189 *Nurture* the effects of education and society on a person. Prospero is saying that, because of Caliban's inherent evil, no amount of teaching or help will make him a better person.

189–90 *pains ... taken* the human care and trouble taken

192 *cankers* decays. *plague* torment

193 *line* a clothesline of rope or a lime or linden tree

194 *blind mole* moles can hear footsteps above their tunnels, though they cannot see them

196 *your fairy* Ariel, who is known to Caliban

197 *jack* trickster

198 *horse piss* all three smell from the 'filthy mantled pool'

202 *lost* ruined, dead

205 *hoodwink* close your eyes to, make you forget. *mischance* accident

206 *hushed as midnight* as still as the middle of the night

213 *fetch off* recover. *o'er ears* over my ears in the slime

215 *good mischief* an oxymoron; the evil deed will serve them well

217 *aye* ever. *foot-licker* slave

PROSPERO   This was well done, my bird.   185
    Thy shape invisible retain thou still;
    The trumpery in my house, go bring it hither,
    For stale to catch these thieves.

ARIEL   I go, I go.   [*Exit*

PROSPERO   A devil, a born devil, on whose nature
    Nurture can never stick; on whom my pains,
    Humanely taken, all, all lost, quite lost;   190
    And as with age his body uglier grows,
    So his mind cankers. I will plague them all,
    Even to roaring.

Enter ARIEL, *loaden with glistering apparel, etc.*

    Come, hang them on this line.

Enter CALIBAN, STEPHANO *and* TRINCULO, *all wet*

CALIBAN   Pray you tread softly, that the blind mole may not
    Hear a foot fall; we now are near his cell.   195

STEPHANO   Monster, your fairy, which you say is a harmless fairy, has done little
better than played the jack with us.

TRINCULO   Monster, I do smell all horse-piss, at which my nose is in great
indignation.

STEPHANO   So is mine. Do you hear, monster? If I should take a displeasure   200
against you, look you, –

TRINCULO   Thou wert but a lost monster.

CALIBAN   Good my lord, give me thy favour still.
    Be patient, for the prize I'll bring thee to
    Shall hoodwink this mischance; therefore speak softly;   205
    All's hushed as midnight yet.

TRINCULO   Ay, but to lose our bottles in the pool –

STEPHANO   There is not only disgrace and dishonour in that, monster, but an
infinite loss.

TRINCULO   That's more to me than my wetting; yet this is your harmless fairy,   210
monster.

STEPHANO   I will fetch off my bottle, though I be o'er ears for my labour.

CALIBAN   Prithee, my King, be quiet. Seest thou here,
    This is the mouth o' the cell: no noise, and enter.
    Do that good mischief which may make this island   215
    Thine own for ever, and I, thy Caliban,
    For aye thy foot-licker.

STEPHANO   Give me thy hand; I do begin to have bloody thoughts.

219 *King … peer* The ballad 'King Stephen was a worthy peer' links clothing to social status.

222 *a frippery* a shop which sold old clothing

223 *gown* a garment evidently more befitting the kingly Stephano

224 *Thy Grace* an appropriate way to address a king

225 *dropsy* a disease which traps watery fluids in the body

226 *luggage* goods generally, here worthless things

230 *Mistress line* Stephano addresses and personifies the line of clothes or an item on it. *jerkin* leather jacket

231–2 *jerkin under … bald jerkin* the line is the equator, on crossing which sailors were believed to go bald; or the body below the waist, where loss of hair suggests syphilis

233 *Do, do* bravo. Trinculo appreciates his friend's wit.
line plumb line. *level* carpenter's level. *an't like* if it pleases

235 *Steal by … level* the proverb means that they are excellent craftsmen in their stealing

236 *pass of pate* thrust of the head, witticism

237 *lime* birdlime, sticky substance to make thieving easier

239 *on't* of it

240 *barnacles* hard-shelled sea creatures or the barnacled goose

241 *villainous* vilely

242 *lay to* bring into action

243 *Go to* get moving

> What would you have Stephano and Trinculo do on stage to maximise the comedy of this part of the scene?
>
> How might the actor playing Caliban show the fear, tension and annoyance at these antics?

S.D. *divers* several different sorts. *setting* urging

246–8 *Mountain, Silver, Fury, Tyrant* the names of the spirit hounds

249 *charge* order. *goblins* mischievous spirits. *grind* torment

250 *convulsions* cramps. *shorten* contract, pull. *sinews* tendons, nerves

251 *pinch-spotted* bruises from pinches

252 *pard … cat o' … mountain* panther or other spotted animal

| TRINCULO | O King Stephano, O peer, O worthy Stephano, look what a wardrobe |
| | here is for thee! | 220 |

| CALIBAN | Let it alone, thou fool, it is but trash. |

| TRINCULO | O ho, monster! we know what belongs to a frippery. O King Stephano! |

| STEPHANO | Put off that gown, Trinculo; by this hand, I'll have that gown. |

| TRINCULO | Thy Grace shall have it. |

CALIBAN	The dropsy drown this fool! What do you mean	225
	To dote thus on such luggage? Let's alone
	And do the murder first: if he awake,
	From toe to crown he'll fill our skins with pinches,
	Make us strange stuff.

STEPHANO	Be you quiet, monster. Mistress line, is not this my jerkin? Now is	230
	the jerkin under the line; now, jerkin, you are like to lose your hair, and
	prove a bald jerkin.

| TRINCULO | Do, do; we steal by line and level, and't like your Grace. |

STEPHANO	I thank thee for that jest; here's a garment for't; wit shall not go
	unrewarded while I am King of this country. 'Steal by line and level' is	235
	an excellent pass of pate; there's another garment for't.

| TRINCULO | Monster, come put some lime upon your fingers, and away with the |
| | rest. |

CALIBAN	I will have none on't: we shall lose our time,
	And all be turned to barnacles, or to apes	240
	With foreheads villainous low.

| STEPHANO | Monster, lay-to your fingers: help to bear this away, where my |
| | hogshead of wine is, or I'll turn you out of my kingdom: go to, carry this. |

| TRINCULO | And this. |

| STEPHANO | Ay, and this. | 245 |

A noise of hunters heard. Enter divers SPIRITS *in shape of dogs and hounds,*
hunting them about; PROSPERO *and* ARIEL *setting them on*

| PROSPERO | Hey, Mountain, hey! |

| ARIEL | Silver! there it goes, Silver. |

| PROSPERO | Fury, Fury! there, Tyrant, there! hark, hark! |

[*Exeunt* CALIBAN, STEPHANO *and* TRINCULO, *pursued by the* SPIRITS

Go, charge my goblins that they grind their joints
With dry convulsions, shorten up their sinews | 250
With agèd cramps, and more pinch-spotted make them
Than pard or cat o' mountain.

253 *soundly* severely

254 *Lies* are subject to, are inactive

256 *have … freedom* possess the air when you are free. *for a little* for a while longer

> The scene should end with noise and confusion. How might you make the most of the hounds? (One production used crocodiles!)
>
> How might film or back-projection, together with stereo sound be effective?

Prospero says, **At this hour / Lies at my mercy all mine enemies**. Write a brief account of what Prospero has done since the ship split. What do you think has been his most important achievement?

This act, unusually, has only one scene, despite the fact that there are two very distinct focuses of action, the masque and the comic thwarting of Caliban's plan.

By the end of the scene, Prospero has moved all of his enemies towards his cell, where he will dispense retribution and forgiveness.

ARIEL   Hark, they roar.

PROSPERO   Let them be hunted soundly. At this hour
            Lies at my mercy all mine enemies;
            Shortly shall all my labours end, and thou   **255**
            Shalt have the air at freedom; for a little
            Follow, and do me service.

                                                    [*Exeunt*

5:1

Prospero reveals himself, as Duke of Milan, to the bewildered courtiers; he forgives them and then discloses Ferdinand and Miranda. The mariners are released and Trinculo, Sebastian and Caliban are led in to complete the party.

Caliban and Ariel are set free from their bondage and, in the Epilogue, Prospero requests the same of the audience.

1	*project* plan; in alchemy, the casting of powders. *gather … head* in alchemy the boiling of ingredients
2	*crack* in alchemy this is over-boiling resulting in failure
3	*Goes … carriage* not overburdened with anxiety. *How's the day?* What time is it?
4	*On* approaching
8	*In … charge* exactly as you ordered
10	*line-grove* a group of lime or linden trees. *weather-fends* defends from bad weather, shelters
11	*till your release* until you release them
12	*abide* stay. *distracted* confused
16	*winter's drops* drops of cold rain
17	*eaves of reeds* thatched roofs
18	*affections* passions, mood
21	*a touch* a sense
23–4	*relish … they* feel emotion just as deeply as they
24	*kindlier moved* more compassionately affected
25	*high wrongs* great crimes. *struck … quick* deeply injured
27	*rarer* more unusual and more noble
28	*virtue* forgiveness, mercy
29	*drift* object
31	*My … break* I'll release them from my magic spell

Which words concerned with alchemy does Prospero use here?

What stage props might you use to illustrate Prospero the alchemist?

What might Ariel do on stage as the alchemist's assistant?

33	*standing lakes* still waters
34	*printless* elves leave no footprints
35	*ebbing* receding. *Neptune* sea – Neptune is the god of the sea. *fly* run from
36	*demi-puppets* half-sized, dwarfish, ie fairy, elf
37	*green sour ringlets* rings that appear at the base of toadstools, made by dancing fairies

108

5:1   *Enter* PROSPERO *in his magic robes, and* ARIEL

PROSPERO   Now does my project gather to a head:
                 My charms crack not, my spirits obey, and Time
                 Goes upright with his carriage. How's the day?

ARIEL   On the sixth hour, at which time, my lord,
                 You said our work should cease.

PROSPERO   I did say so,   **5**
                 When first I raised the tempest. Say, my spirit,
                 How fares the King and's followers?

ARIEL   Confined together
                 In the same fashion as you gave in charge,
                 Just as you left them; all prisoners, sir,
                 In the line-grove which weather-fends your cell;   **10**
                 They cannot budge till your release. The King,
                 His brother, and yours, abide all three distracted,
                 And the remainder mourning over them,
                 Brimful of sorrow and dismay; but chiefly
                 Him that you termed, sir, 'the good old lord Gonzalo,'   **15**
                 His tears run down his beard like winter's drops
                 From eaves of reeds. Your charm so strongly works 'em
                 That, if you now beheld them, your affections
                 Would become tender.

PROSPERO   Dost thou think so, spirit?

ARIEL   Mine would, sir, were I human.

PROSPERO   And mine shall.   **20**
                 Hast thou, which art but air, a touch, a feeling
                 Of their afflictions, and shall not myself,
                 One of their kind, that relish all as sharply
                 Passion as they, be kindlier moved than thou art?
                 Though with their high wrongs I am struck to the quick, **25**
                 Yet with my nobler reason 'gainst my fury
                 Do I take part. The rarer action is
                 In virtue than in vengeance. They being penitent,
                 The sole drift of my purpose doth extend
                 Not a frown further: go, release them, Ariel.   **30**
                 My charms I'll break, their senses I'll restore,
                 And they shall be themselves.

ARIEL   I'll fetch them, sir.   [*Exit*

PROSPERO   Ye elves of hills, brooks, standing lakes, and groves,
                 And ye that on the sands with printless foot
                 Do chase the ebbing Neptune, and do fly him   **35**
                 When he comes back; you demi-puppets that
                 By moonshine do the green sour ringlets make,

38	*ewe not bites*	sheep will not eat the 'sour grass'
39	*midnight mushrooms*	mushrooms that spring up overnight
40	*solemn curfew*	the 9 o'clock bell, which set spirits and fairies free to roam the earth till sunrise

38 *ewe not bites* sheep will not eat the 'sour grass'

39 *midnight mushrooms* mushrooms that spring up overnight

40 *solemn curfew* the 9 o'clock bell, which set spirits and fairies free to roam the earth till sunrise

41 *Weak masters* ministers or agents of Prospero with some power of their own. *bedimmed* made dim, eclipsed

42 *mutinous winds* winds that can cause trouble

43 *azured vault* the sky

44 *roaring war* such as a tempest

45 *fire* lightning. *rifted* split. *Jove's stout oak* the oak was sacred to Jove

46 *bolt* thunderbolt. *strong-based ... promontory* broad-based, secure hill or headland

47 *spurs* roots

49 *waked their sleepers* raised their dead. *oped* opened

50 *potent* powerful. *rough magic* magic used for violent ends; raising the dead was, in fact, black magic

51 *abjure* renounce, give up. *required* demanded

54 *airy charm* the 'heavenly music'. *break my staff* break and bury his magic staff, destroy his power

55 *fathoms* a fathom is 6 feet

56 *plummet* a plumb line, which measures the depth of water

57 *book* book of magical arts.

S.D. *charmed* spellbound. *Prospero observing* Prospero is outside the circle and invisible until line 106.

How would you have Prospero trace his magic circle at line 33?

How might Ariel move the courtiers into the circle? Perhaps with dance and music? – remember they are 'spellbound'.

What does Alonso's **frantic gesture** look like? What are the others doing?

59 *unsettled fancy* troubled imagination. *thy* Prospero is here addressing Alonso.

60 *boiled* a reference to alchemy – the fact that Alonso is spellbound

61 *spell-stopped* under a spell

63 *sociable* sympathetic

64 *fellowly drops* companionable tears – in fellowship *apace* speedily

66 *rising senses* the senses of the courtiers are returning as the spell breaks

67 *chase* chase away. *ignorant fumes* things they do not understand. *mantle* cover

69 *sir* gentleman

70 *him* Alonso

70–1 *pay ... Home* proverbial; to repay a debt completely

74 *pinched* tormented

75 *entertained* harboured

76 *Expelled ... nature* rejected natural feelings

77 *inward pinches* mental torment, anguish

Whereof the ewe not bites; and you whose pastime
Is to make midnight mushrooms, that rejoice
To hear the solemn curfew, by whose aid   **40**
(Weak masters though ye be) I have bedimmed
The noontide sun, called forth the mutinous winds,
And 'twixt the green sea and the azured vault
Set roaring war; to the dread rattling thunder
Have I given fire, and rifted Jove's stout oak   **45**
With his own bolt; the strong-based promontory
Have I made shake, and by the spurs plucked up
The pine and cedar; graves at my command
Have waked their sleepers, oped, and let 'em forth
By my so potent Art. But this rough magic   **50**
I here abjure: and when I have required
Some heavenly music – which even now I do –
To work mine end upon their senses, that
This airy charm is for, I'll break my staff,
Bury it certain fathoms in the earth,   **55**
And deeper than did ever plummet sound
I'll drown my book.

Solemn music. Here enters **ARIEL** *before; then* **ALONSO** *with a frantic gesture,
attended by* **GONZALO**; **SEBASTIAN** *and* **ANTONIO** *in like manner, attended by*
ADRIAN *and* **FRANCISCO**: *they all enter the circle which* **PROSPERO** *had made,
and there stand charmed; which* **PROSPERO** *observing, speaks*

A solemn air, and the best comforter
To an unsettled fancy, cure thy brains,
Now useless, boiled within thy skull! There stand,   **60**
For you are spell-stopped.
Holy Gonzalo, honourable man,
Mine eyes, even sociable to the show of thine,
Fall fellowly drops. The charm dissolves apace,
And as the morning steals upon the night,   **65**
Melting the darkness, so their rising senses
Begin to chase the ignorant fumes that mantle
Their clearer reason. O good Gonzalo,
My true preserver, and a loyal sir
To him thou follow'st, I will pay thy graces   **70**
Home, both in word and deed. Most cruelly
Didst thou, Alonso, use me and my daughter;
Thy brother was a furtherer in the act;
Thou art pinched for't now, Sebastian. Flesh and blood,
You, brother mine, that entertained ambition,   **75**
Expelled remorse and nature, who, with Sebastian –
Whose inward pinches therefore are most strong –
Would here have killed your King; I do forgive thee,
Unnatural though thou art. Their understanding

111

80 *swell* grow. *tide* the oncoming sense of consciousness and realisation

81 *reasonable shore* the level of their reason, understanding

84 *rapier* sword worn by a gentleman

85 *discase* undress

86 *sometime Milan* previously Duke of Milan

What is Prospero's mood during his speech between lines 58 and 83? Does his tone of voice change? How many different people is he talking to?

How would you have Prospero move about during this speech?

How would you ensure that the actor makes the complex imagery in this scene clear to the audience?

---

89 *cowslip bell* the bell shape of the flower

90 *couch* crouch

92 *After* pursuing

96 *so, so, so* Prospero appreciatively adjusts his attire as Duke of Milan.

99 *Under the hatches* below deck

100 *Being awake* when they have been woken. *enforce them* use your power to bring them

101 *presently* immediately

102 *I ... me* I devour the way, I travel quickly

103 *Or ere* before

105 *Inhabits* lives

106 *fearful* terrifying

108 *For more assurance* for further proof

111 *Whe'er* whether

112 *enchanted trifle* magic trick. *abuse* mistreat

115 *affliction* confusion, madness. *amends* heals, gets better

116 *crave* demand, require

117 *And if* if indeed. *be at all* be really happening

118 *Thy dukedom* the duchy of Milan which, by agreement with Antonio, Naples controls

119 *how should* how can it be that

What does Prospero say which prompts Ariel to sing?

Plot Ariel's movements as he sings – remember he can fly.

What is Ariel's song about? Make up music for it, to fit the mood.

	Begins to swell, and the approaching tide	80
	Will shortly fill the reasonable shore,	
	That now lies foul and muddy – not one of them	
	That yet looks on me, or would know me. Ariel,	
	Fetch me the hat and rapier in my cell;	
	I will discase me, and myself present	85
	As I was sometime Milan. Quickly, spirit;	
	Thou shalt ere long be free.	

ARIEL sings and helps to attire him

	Where the bee sucks, there suck I;	
	In a cowslip's bell I lie;	
	There I couch when owls do cry;	90
	On the bat's back I do fly	
	After summer merrily.	
	Merrily, merrily, shall I live now,	
	Under the blossom that hangs on the bough.	

PROSPERO	Why, that's my dainty Ariel. I shall miss thee,	95
	But yet thou shalt have freedom; so, so, so.	
	To the King's ship, invisible as thou art;	
	There shalt thou find the mariners asleep	
	Under the hatches: the Master and the Boatswain	
	Being awake, enforce them to this place,	100
	And presently, I prithee.	

ARIEL	I drink the air before me, and return	
	Or ere your pulse twice beat.	

[Exit

GONZALO	All torment, trouble, wonder and amazement	
	Inhabits here: some heavenly power guide us	105
	Out of this fearful country!	

PROSPERO	Behold, Sir King,	
	The wrongèd Duke of Milan, Prospero!	
	For more assurance that a living prince	
	Does now speak to thee, I embrace thy body;	
	And to thee and thy company I bid	110
	A hearty welcome.	

ALONSO	Whe'er thou beest he or no,	
	Or some enchanted trifle to abuse me,	
	As late I have been, I not know; thy pulse	
	Beats as of flesh and blood; and, since I saw thee,	
	Th'affliction of my mind amends, with which	115
	I fear a madness held me. This must crave,	
	And if this be at all, a most strange story.	
	Thy Dukedom I resign, and do entreat	
	Thou pardon me my wrongs; but how should Prospero	
	Be living, and be here?	

121   *thine age*   Gonzalo is elderly

122   *confined*   has no limit

123–4   *You … isle*   you are still under the influence of magic

125   *my friends all*   a general statement of goodwill

126   *brace*   pair

127   *pluck*   bring down

128   *justify*   prove

132   *require*   demand

133   *perforce*   of necessity

135   *particulars*   details

136   *since*   ago

139   *woe for't*   sorry

141   *past her cure*   beyond the cure of patience

142   *soft*   compassionate

143   *like loss*   similar loss.   *her sovereign aid*   the potent help of patience

145   *late*   recent

145–7   *supportable … comfort you*   Prospero is saying that he has fewer means to comfort him in his grief than Alonso has.

146   *dear*   severe, grievous.   *means much weaker*   Prospero may mean that the loss of his daughter leaves him alone and solitary, whereas Alonso, as a king with royal privileges and distractions, as well as a daughter, Claribel, has many more compensations for his grief.

148   *lost my daughter*   by her betrothal to Ferdinand

150   *That*   provided that, if only

151   *mudded*   buried in the mud.   *oozy bed*   the ocean floor

154   *do so much admire*   are so full of awe

PROSPERO [*To* GONZALO]   First, noble friend, **120**
    Let me embrace thine age, whose honour cannot
    Be measured or confined.

GONZALO   Whether this be,
    Or be not, I'll not swear.

PROSPERO   You do yet taste
    Some subtleties o' th' isle, that will not let you
    Believe things certain. Welcome, my friends all. **125**
    [*To* SEBASTIAN *and* ANTONIO] But you, my brace of lords, were I so minded,
    I here could pluck his Highness' frown upon you
    And justify you traitors. At this time
    I will tell no tales.

SEBASTIAN   The Devil speaks in him.

PROSPERO   No.
    For you, most wicked sir, whom to call brother **130**
    Would even infect my mouth, I do forgive
    Thy rankest fault – all of them – and require
    My Dukedom of thee, which perforce I know
    Thou must restore.

ALONSO   If thou beest Prospero,
    Give us particulars of thy preservation, **135**
    How thou hast met us here, who three hours since
    Were wracked upon this shore? where I have lost –
    How sharp the point of this remembrance is –
    My dear son Ferdinand.

PROSPERO   I am woe for't, sir.

ALONSO   Irreparable is the loss, and Patience **140**
    Says it is past her cure.

PROSPERO   I rather think
    You have not sought her help, of whose soft grace
    For the like loss, I have her sovereign aid,
    And rest myself content.

ALONSO   You the like loss?

PROSPERO   As great to me, as late; and, supportable **145**
    To make the dear loss, have I means much weaker
    Than you may call to comfort you; for I
    Have lost my daughter.

ALONSO   A daughter?
    O heavens, that they were living both in Naples,
    The King and Queen there! That they were, I wish **150**
    Myself were mudded in that oozy bed
    Where my son lies. When did you lose your daughter?

PROSPERO   In this last tempest. I perceive these lords
    At this encounter do so much admire

155 *devour their reason* their reason is swallowed up

156 *do offices of truth* tell the truth

157 *natural breath* ordinary speech

160 *of* from. *strangely* in an extraordinary way

163 *chronicle* account, story. *of day by day* either of daily events, or to be told over many days

164 *relation* report

167 *abroad* elsewhere

169 *requite* reward

170 *wonder* a pun on Miranda's name

172 *you play me false* you are cheating

174 *score* twenty. *wrangle* argue, dispute

176 *vision* illusion

177 *twice lose* the second being when the vision disappears

180 *compass* encircle, embrace

186 *eld'st* longest

> *How would you make the 'discovery' of Ferdinand and Miranda dramatic on stage: with a curtain, by the use of lighting, some advanced computer technology?*

Sweet lord, you play me false.

That they devour their reason, and scarce think   **155**
Their eyes do offices of truth, their words
Are natural breath; but howsoe'er you have
Been jostled from your senses, know for certain
That I am Prospero, and that very Duke
Which was thrust forth of Milan; who most strangely   **160**
Upon this shore where you were wracked was landed,
To be the lord on't. No more yet of this,
For 'tis a chronicle of day by day,
Not a relation for a breakfast, nor
Befitting this first meeting. Welcome, sir;   **165**
This cell's my court; here have I few attendants,
And subjects none abroad. Pray you, look in:
My Dukedom since you have given me again,
I will requite you with as good a thing,
At least bring forth a wonder, to content ye   **170**
As much as me my Dukedom.

Here PROSPERO *discovers* FERDINAND *and* MIRANDA *playing at chess*

MIRANDA   Sweet lord, you play me false.

FERDINAND   No, my dearest love,
    I would not for the world.

MIRANDA   Yes, for a score of kingdoms, you should wrangle,
    And I would call it fair play.

ALONSO   If this prove   **175**
    A vision of the island, one dear son
    Shall I twice lose.

SEBASTIAN   A most high miracle.

FERDINAND [*Having seen* ALONSO] Though the seas threaten, they are merciful;
    I have cursed them without cause.

Kneels before ALONSO

ALONSO   Now all the blessings
    Of a glad father compass thee about!   **180**
    Arise, and say how thou cam'st here.

MIRANDA   O wonder!
    How many goodly creatures are there here!
    How beauteous mankind is! O brave new world
    That has such people in't.

PROSPERO   'Tis new to thee.

ALONSO   What is this maid, with whom thou wast at play?   **185**
    Your eld'st acquaintance cannot be three hours.
    Is she the goddess that hath severed us,
    And brought us thus together?

191   *advice*   advice and also permission to marry

193   *renown*   report

194   *of whom*   from whom

195   *second father*   father-in-law

196   *I am hers*   Miranda's father-in-law

199   *burden*   weigh down

200   *heaviness*   sadness, grief.   *inly*   inwardly

203   *chalked forth*   marked out

205   *Was Milan … Milan*   was the Duke of Milan forced from the city of Milan

208   *pillars*   monuments

213   *was his own*   knew himself, was in control of himself

214   *still*   forever

*On line 198, Prospero seems to interrupt Alonso with the words **There, sir, stop**. What might Alonso be doing?*

*What might Gonzalo's **pillars** look like?*

218   *Blasphemy*   you who blaspheme, the boatswain

219   *swears't … overboard*   that swears enough to drive 'grace' overboard

220   *no mouth*   nothing to say

223   *three glasses*   three hours.   *gave out*   reported

224   *tight and yare*   ship-shape, seaworthy.   *bravely*   finely

FERDINAND   Sir, she is mortal;
        But by immortal Providence she's mine.
        I chose her when I could not ask my father   190
        For his advice, nor thought I had one. She
        Is daughter to this famous Duke of Milan,
        Of whom so often I have heard renown,
        But never saw before; of whom I have
        Received a second life; and second father   195
        This lady makes him to me.

ALONSO   I am hers.
        But O, how oddly will it sound, that I
        Must ask my child forgiveness!

PROSPERO   There, sir, stop.
        Let us not burden our remembrances with
        A heaviness that's gone.

GONZALO   I have inly wept,   200
        Or should have spoke ere this. Look down, you gods,
        And on this couple drop a blessèd crown;
        For it is you that have chalked forth the way
        Which brought us hither.

ALONSO   I say amen, Gonzalo.

GONZALO   Was Milan thrust from Milan, that his issue   205
        Should become Kings of Naples? O rejoice
        Beyond a common joy, and set it down
        With gold on lasting pillars. In one voyage
        Did Claribel her husband find at Tunis,
        And Ferdinand, her brother, found a wife,   210
        Where he himself was lost; Prospero, his Dukedom
        In a poor isle; and all of us, ourselves,
        When no man was his own.

ALONSO [*To* FERDINAND *and* MIRANDA] Give me your hands;
        Let grief and sorrow still embrace his heart
        That doth not wish you joy.

GONZALO   Be it so, amen.   215

        Enter ARIEL, *with the* MASTER *and* BOATSWAIN *amazedly following*

        O look, sir, look, sir, here is more of us.
        I prophesied, if a gallows were on land
        This fellow could not drown. Now, Blasphemy,
        That swear'st grace o'erboard, not an oath on shore?
        Hast thou no mouth by land? What is the news?   220

BOATSWAIN The best news is that we have safely found
        Our King and company; the next, our ship,
        Which but three glasses since we gave out split,
        Is tight and yare, and bravely rigged as when
        We first put out to sea.

119

226   *tricksy* clever

227–8 *strengthen ... stranger* grow more and more strange

230   *dead of sleep* in a deep sleep

231   *clapped under hatches* confined below deck

232   *even now* just recently. *several* different

234   *mo diversity* more variety

236   *all her trim* properly fitted out for sailing

237   *gallant* stately

238   *Capering* dancing joyfully. *on a trice* in an instant

240   *moping* bewildered

241   *Diligence* diligent one

244   *conduct* conductor, director

244–5 *oracle ... knowledge* some wise person must explain these strange events to us

Read the Boatswain's speech on lines 229–40. Improvise the dream, awakening and the **brought moping hither**.

How would you have the Master **Capering?** The mood of the actions are comic, reflecting the happy outcome.

246   *infest* trouble. *beating* hammering out, trying to explain

247   *picked leisure* chosen spare time

248   *shortly* soon. *single* on your own, privately

249   *probable* provable, believable

250   *accidents* events

256–7 *Every man ... Fortune* proverbial; but Stephano, being drunk, has reversed the sense of 'Every man for himself'

257   *Coragio* have courage. *bully* gallant

258   *true spies* eyes that tell the truth

259   *Setebos* Caliban's god. *brave* wonderful, splendid

260   *fine* finely dressed, smart

ARIEL	Sir, all this service	225

Have I done since I went.

PROSPERO   My tricksy spirit!

ALONSO   These are not natural events, they strengthen
        From strange to stranger; say, how came you hither?

BOATSWAIN If I did think, sir, I were well awake,
        I'd strive to tell you. We were dead of sleep,   230
        And – how we know not – all clapped under hatches,
        Where, but even now, with strange and several noises
        Of roaring, shrieking, howling, jingling chains,
        And mo diversity of sounds, all horrible,
        We were awaked; straightway, at liberty;   235
        Where we, in all her trim, freshly beheld
        Our royal, good, and gallant ship; our Master
        Capering to eye her; on a trice, so please you,
        Even in a dream, were we divided from them,
        And were brought moping hither.

ARIEL   Was't well done?   240

PROSPERO   Bravely, my Diligence; thou shalt be free.

ALONSO   This is as strange a maze as e'er men trod,
        And there is in this business more than nature
        Was ever conduct of: some oracle
        Must rectify our knowledge.

PROSPERO   Sir, my liege,   245
        Do not infest your mind with beating on
        The strangeness of this business; at picked leisure,
        Which shall be shortly single, I'll resolve you,
        Which to you shall seem probable, of every
        These happened accidents; till when, be cheerful   250
        And think of each thing well. Come hither, spirit;
        Set Caliban and his companions free;
        Untie the spell. How fares my gracious sir?   [*Exit* ARIEL
        There are yet missing of your company
        Some few odd lads that you remember not.   255

    Enter ARIEL, *driving in* CALIBAN, STEPHANO, *and* TRINCULO, *in their stolen apparel*

STEPHANO   Every man shift for all the rest, and let no man take care for himself,
        for all is but Fortune. Coragio, bully-monster, coragio!

TRINCULO   If these be true spies which I wear in my head, here's a goodly sight.

CALIBAN   O Setebos, these be brave spirits indeed:
        How fine my master is! I am afraid   260
        He will chastise me.

SEBASTIAN   Ha, ha!
        What things are these, my lord Antonio?
        Will money buy 'em?

264 *plain fish* a reference to Caliban's smell

265 *badges* insignia of employment – of Alonso's court

266 *true* genuine. *mis-shapen* indicating physical or moral deformity

267 *mother* Sycorax

268 *control … ebbs* had magical power over the moon and therefore the tides

269 *deal … power* Sycorax could usurp the moon's sphere of influence beyond the limits of the moon's power.

270 *robbed me* they are wearing the stolen clothes, the 'glistering apparel'. *demi-devil* Caliban's father was, reputedly, the devil.

271 *bastard* illegitimate or cross-bred

273 *own* acknowledge. *thing of darkness* dark-skinned and of moral depravity

274 *Acknowledge mine* Prospero is explaining that Caliban belongs to him as his slave. *pinched* tormented

277 *reeling ripe* staggering because of drink

278 *liquor* drink but also a reference to 'lixir' in alchemy. *gilded them* flushed their faces; also in alchemy 'turned to gold'

279 *pickle* mess; also the alcohol has turned Trinculo into a pickle

281 *never … bones* he is so saturated with alcohol that it will never leave his bones. *not fear fly-blowing* Flies will only lay eggs on fresh, not pickled, meat.

283 *cramp* ie the suffering Ariel has put upon him

284 *sirrah* a contemptuous address

285 *sore* painful, aching

287 *disproportioned* misshapen, deformed in mind and body. *manners* conduct, morality

289 *look* hope

290 *trim it handsomely* decorate the cell beautifully

292 *grace* mercy, favour. *thrice-double* six-times

294 *worship* honour, respect

295 *luggage* stolen garments

297 *train* followers

299 *waste* pass the time

301 *quick* quickly

122

ANTONIO	Very like; one of them	

ANTONIO   Very like; one of them
    Is a plain fish and no doubt marketable.

PROSPERO   Mark but the badges of these men, my lords,   265
    Then say if they be true. This mis-shapen knave,
    His mother was a witch, and one so strong
    That could control the moon, make flows and ebbs,
    And deal in her command, without her power.
    These three have robbed me; and this demi-devil –   270
    For he's a bastard one – had plotted with them
    To take my life. Two of these fellows you
    Must know and own; this thing of darkness I
    Acknowledge mine.

CALIBAN   I shall be pinched to death.

ALONSO   Is not this Stephano, my drunken butler?   275

SEBASTIAN   He is drunk now; where had he wine?

ALONSO   And Trinculo is reeling ripe; where should they
    Find this grand liquor that hath gilded 'em?
    How cam'st thou in this pickle?

TRINCULO   I have been in such a pickle since I saw you last that I fear me will   280
    never out of my bones. I shall not fear fly-blowing.

SEBASTIAN   Why, how now, Stephano?

STEPHANO   O touch me not, I am not Stephano but a cramp.

PROSPERO   You'd be king o' th' isle, sirrah?

STEPHANO   I should have been a sore one then.   285

ALONSO   This is as strange a thing as e'er I looked on.

PROSPERO   He is as disproportioned in his manners
    As in his shape. Go sirrah, to my cell;
    Take with you your companions. As you look
    To have my pardon, trim it handsomely.   290

CALIBAN   Ay, that I will. And I'll be wise hereafter,
    And seek for grace. What a thrice-double ass
    Was I to take this drunkard for a god
    And worship this dull fool!

PROSPERO   Go to, away.

ALONSO   Hence, and bestow your luggage where you found it.   295

SEBASTIAN   Or stole it rather.

                      [Exeunt CALIBAN, STEPHANO, *and* TRINCULO

PROSPERO   Sir, I invite your Highness and your train
    To my poor cell, where you shall take your rest
    For this one night, which, part of it, I'll waste
    With such discourse as I not doubt shall make it   300
    Go quick away: the story of my life

302 *accidents* events

305 *nuptial* wedding

308 *third thought* Prospero, his task done, will contemplate death as
well as his Dukedom and his daughter.

310 *take the ear* affect, captivate the listener. *deliver all* report
everything

312 *catch* catch up with

313 *my chick* a term of endearment with connotations of flying

*How would you have Caliban speak his last lines and leave the stage? He
should show signs of regret and a desire to* **seek for grace**.

*How might Ariel's departure from Prospero's control be marked? Perhaps with
dance and flight?*

What differences do you find in the rhythm and tone of Prospero's last
speeches with those in Act 1 Scene 2? How would you reflect this in his
attitude on stage?

The play is partly about change and transformation. Who changes the most
and how do they change? Does anybody not change?

*Prospero's project has been realised and the resolution of all the issues and
characters achieved. Prospero used his magic, his power for good. He achieved
reconciliation through forgiveness.*

124

And the particular accidents gone by
Since I came to this isle; and in the morn
I'll bring you to your ship, and so to Naples,
Where I have hope to see the nuptial   305
Of these our dear-belovèd solemnised,
And thence retire me to my Milan, where
Every third thought shall be my grave.

ALONSO   I long
To hear the story of your life, which must
Take the ear strangely.   310

PROSPERO   I'll deliver all,
And promise you calm seas, auspicious gales,
And sail so expeditious that shall catch
Your royal fleet far off. My Ariel! chick,
That is thy charge; then to the elements
Be free and fare thou well! Please you draw near.   315

[Exeunt

EPILOGUE

The Epilogue has no dramatic significance for the play, which is over. It may have been added for special occasions or court performances.

1	*charms … o'erthrown* Prospero's magical powers are relinquished and the actor's role is played
4	*confined by you* the audience may release him or confine him – as he confined others
8	*bare island* the imaginary setting of the play; and the stage
9	*bands* bonds, confinement
10	*good hands* applause; a sudden noise could break a magic spell
11	*Gentle breath* cheers or kind reviews from the audience
12	*project* return to Milan; the actor's aim of pleasing an audience
13	*want* lack
15–16	*ending … prayer* without his Art, Prospero is simply human in need of mercy and forgiveness
17–18	*pierces … faults* prayer can break through to Mercy and receive pardon for all shortcomings
19	*crimes* sins
20	*indulgence* favour, gift; or perhaps a final irreverent pun on the practice of buying forgiveness of sins

The actor playing Prospero refers to **this bare island** on line 8. What would you have happening on stage behind him?

EPILOGUE

Enter **PROSPERO**

PROSPERO   Now my charms are all o'erthrown,
And what strength I have's mine own,
Which is most faint; now, 'tis true,
I must be here confined by you,
Or sent to Naples. Let me not,   5
Since I have my Dukedom got,
And pardoned the deceiver, dwell
In this bare island, by your spell;
But release me from my bands
With the help of your good hands.   10
Gentle breath of yours my sails
Must fill, or else my project fails,
Which was to please. Now I want
Spirits to enforce, art to enchant;
And my ending is despair,   15
Unless I be relieved by prayer,
Which pierces so that it assaults
Mercy itself, and frees all faults.
As you from crimes would pardoned be,
Let your indulgence set me free.   20

                      [*Exit*

List of other titles in this series:

NT Shakespeare: Henry IV Part One
Lawrence Green
0-7487-6960-9

NT Shakespeare: Henry IV Part One Teacher Resource Book
Lawrence Green
0-7487-6968-4

NT Shakespeare: Julius Caesar
Mark Morris
0-7487-6959-5

NT Shakespeare: Julius Caesar Teacher Resource Book
Mark Morris
0-7487-6967-6

NT Shakespeare: Macbeth
Dinah Jurksaitis
0-7487-6955-2

NT Shakespeare: Macbeth Teacher Resource Book
Dinah Jurksaitis
0-7487-6961-7

NT Shakespeare: The Merchant of Venice
Tony Farrell
0-7487-6957-9

NT Shakespeare: The Merchant of Venice Teacher Resource Book
Tony Farrell
0-7487-6963-3

NT Shakespeare: Romeo and Juliet
Duncan Beal
0-7487-6956-0

NT Shakespeare: Romeo and Juliet Teacher Resource Book
Duncan Beal
0-7487-6962-5

NT Shakespeare: The Tempest Teacher Resource Book
David Stone
0-7487-6965-X